THE
DEAD
ARE
GODS

THE DEAD ARE GODS

a memoir

EIRINIE CARSON

MELVILLE HOUSE

BROOKLYN • LONDON

THE DEAD ARE GODS

First published April 2023 by Melville House
Copyright © Eirinie Carson, 2022
All rights reserved
First Melville House Printing: February 2023

Melville House Publishing
46 John Street
Brooklyn, NY 11201

and

Melville House UK
Suite 2000
16/18 Woodford Road
London E7 0HA

mhpbooks.com
@melvillehouse

ISBN: 978-1-68589-045-2
ISBN: 978-1-68589-046-9 (eBook)

Library of Congress Control Number 2022949070

Designed by Beste M. Dogan

Printed in the United States of America
10 9 8 7 6 5 4 3 2 1

A catalog record for this book is available from the Library of Congress

This book, like everything I do,
is for Luka and Selah.

"As we speak our hearts in mourning we
share our intimate knowledge of the dead, of who
they were and how they lived."
—bell hooks

"Grief is the terrible reminder of the depths
of our love and, like love, grief is non-negotiable."
—NICK CAVE

M y best friend, Larissa, died three years ago. A sudden death, improbable and unexpected. She died a week after my thirty-first birthday, two weeks after her thirty-second. A vibrant human, also improbable and unexpected: a cool rock-and-roll type with a love of poetry. An enigma, hard to gain a grip on, a mythical woman, indulgent, reverent. Loved by us all.

But this is not a eulogy. This is not a chapter to describe to you her love of Charlie Parker and Rimbaud and also, somehow, *Gilmore Girls*. Her deep love of Slipknot and wrestling but also of Baudelaire and good wine. Not a chapter to try to show you, dear stranger, the true person you have lost without even knowing you had her. But how do we discuss grief without eulogising the people we have lost?

Roughly 3.5 million people died in 2021 in the United States alone. Think of that. Think of the mothers and fathers, friends, sponsors, colleagues affected by those deaths. Think of the ripple effect from each one. We are all in mourning, all of us, but ironically, the grief feels so personal, so lonely.

If someone you knew and loved has died, you know the echoing sentiments of it all too well. You know the platitudes your friends and family and (if you are lucky) therapists tell you—grief comes in waves, the only way out is through, you have to be strong for your family/their family/yourself, time heals, you must keep busy. All impossible to soak in and even more impossible to imagine implementing.

You know the obsessiveness—weeks spent poring over the minutiae of the days and hours prior to death, as if somewhere, hidden in plain sight, is the answer. Something you missed that could have prevented it all. For me, it was cross-examining our texts, searching for an arrow that would say, "Look, here is her looming death. Here it is." Dissecting past conversations with mutual friends, searching for anything that would make us understand that it was unavoidable. It is a funny instinct. Why would we want proof that we could not save our loves? Why would we want to feel powerless? Perhaps only to quieten the thoughts that we could have done something, to prove that this was inevitable, that they could not be helped.

Larissa died in the bath. An accident, we were told. The week she died (although at the time we only thought her missing), my toddler had put my husband's phone in her bath in the split second I turned my back whilst I went to fetch her towels. That week was also the one in which I experienced terrible vertigo for the first time, in which I said to my husband "I'm not exaggerating when

I say I might be dying." I also suddenly desired to listen to 1940s jazz, Thelonious Monk, Dizzy Gillespie, and Bud Powell, some of Larry's favourites. All of these things are now, in hindsight, signs. Signs she was dead.

The pain of grief is staggering. The sheer depths of it unfathomable. A tightening in the chest, an inescapable flood of sadness, the sudden need to sit up and cry. All-consuming, this pain. True, there are instances in which people claim to be fine, to be processing it all well. You yourself may be thinking, "I haven't cried once since X died and I went back to work the following day." Well, let me be your harbinger. Let me stand over you and tell you it is coming. It is un-outrun-able, we cannot be strong against it. It is a tsunami, ready to plow through your life with impunity. Maybe not for months and maybe not for years but it will be here.

Doesn't that sound terrifying?

Well, I am also here to tell you that to allow yourself to feel it, to stand in its dark waters, to feel the wet and cold seeping through your clothes, is to weather the storm. Because when it passes (which it will, it comes in waves, remember?), clarity will come in its place. A calmness, an acceptance. The ability to recall details of your person. The way she laughed perhaps, or stood close and asked, "Are we best friends?" even though she knew the answer.

Nothing has been permanent in these short (but somehow long, how does that work?) months. No feeling, no sentiment. Only her absence, I suppose. We cannot sidestep this pain, only weather it, like love, like life, like it all.

I continue to grieve, and will forever, for as long as I can remember her. Time won't heal it completely but it will dull the edges of my grief, sharp and jagged and lethal as they are now. For that is what remembrance is—grieving but with the added caveat of acceptance. Hold Death close. Feel the pain and the nuances of your sadness. Remember those you loved. Say their names and tell their stories.

Her name was Larissa.

The only way out is through.

Eirinie <eirinieeee@xmail.com >   Jun 7, 2014,
to Larissa   7:13 PM

You're my soulmate, do you know that?

—

Sent from my iPad

Larissa <larry67@xmail.com>   Jun 8, 2014,
to me   3:50 AM

Of course I know that.

THE DAY AFTER ·

A blur. Not just one of those things you say, but really, truly, a blur. My eyes cannot focus on the plate of food Adam pushes towards me, I cannot remember getting dressed but somehow I am. My child tugs me down to the floor to play with her trains and there is some peace in that—clicking the little wooden tracks together, slotting them in place, making sure they bend and turn back towards each other, making a circle. Magnetic trains one after another, tiny hands at my aid.

My phone rings and I am back, back to that gnawing at my chest, back to the dropping of my heart. I pick it up, yet another person urging me to confirm what I can barely look at. I am outside now, sitting on the steps of our LA house looking out onto the front yard. The artichokes, their jagged edges, the green, my mind drifting to harvesting them for dinner, but I suddenly can't remember how to cook them. Back to the voice at the end of the line, they are crying and it makes my tears dry instantly. I listen to them objectively, thinking how sad they sound, how distraught. I enjoy it. I am horrified that I enjoy it. That I like hearing this. Later I will reflect, realise that it was enjoyable to hear someone else in the throes of grief, confirming the worst. It was life-affirming to me, but at that moment I cannot clearly see this so I vacillate between the joy at their racked sobs and disgust at myself that I can bathe so deeply in someone else's misery.

I find this so addictive that at the end of this call I find myself making another one, and another. I enjoy breaking the news to people, I enjoy hearing their pause, their contention with whether this is fact or fiction, I enjoy being told "I am so sorry, Eirinie." I want them to be sorry, I want them to pity me because I pity me and I know no other way to be right now.

The sun is setting and Adam comes to tell me there is food inside, if I like. He reassures me he will do our child's bedtime routine; he wants me to know I can have all the time in the world. Do I want to run, he asks? A walk maybe? I cannot even muster the strength to tell him how tired I am, how I couldn't run even if I wanted to and I do want to, I want to run far and long until my chest aches from something other than sadness, until my legs no longer move from something other than a paralyzing sorrow, until my head is clear and all I can hear is my own breath, in and out, in and out. But I don't. I push past him, back inside. I can't remember if I have answered him but as I fall back into bed I think, let this be my answer.

I sleep for an hour and when I awake the toddler is asleep. Adam is timid in his question and he seems to be unable to stop himself from asking, "Are you all right?"

"Can I have some wine?" I say, and he is up and pouring a glass immediately, grateful to help.

He knew her too, I think to myself. He knew her well. She was there when we met at the Standard on Sunset, he watched her exhale her cigarette smoke by the pool, her eyes watching us together as if already viewing the future we could not yet see. Mystical. He knew her when he would come to visit me in the UK, stay for three weeks in our small North London apartment, buy us cocktails when we went out, buy us takeout when we stayed in. He knew her. They had gone on walks to the pub alone together, they had discussed music and bands and rock and roll together. He had been the jury to her in-home fashion shows, told her which dress looked best so that she inevitably picked the other dress he hadn't mentioned. He had been blessed with a nickname, "A." Simple, yes, but an honour from Larissa. A badge of inclusion, a sign that he was down. He knew her too.

And yet I can't think of his pain and loss, there is no fucking space in this house for both of our tears. There is no space. Despite my relishing other people's sorrow down a phone line I refuse to let Adam cry, I cannot bear witness to that. My grief lives here now and there is no fucking room.

I drink a lot that night. I play her voice notes and I cry, too loudly for someone with a young baby in the house. I call her phone even though I know it is in police custody. Somewhere within me, somehow, there is a part that defies logic. I steel myself to hear her voice on the other end, and every time I do not, I am surprised.

You know that burning feeling in your eyes when you have been crying too long? That trite little phrase "I am all cried out"? How true those words ring at three in the morning when I am drunk and forlorn and devastated but unable to muster one single emotion. Adam takes me into bed, I assume, I don't remember how but suddenly that's where I am. Adam's care of me barely registers. It will only be much later that I will mull it over and think of all the little things he did to keep me alive.

Fragmented sentences to Adam. I am writing a history book with my words; I am relegating her to the past tense. I get out half a tale about her before I stop, I cannot finish it. I cannot finish the story because to finish it would be to set it in stone, to cement her as a relic and a character instead of the flesh-and-blood person I want to keep believing she is.

....

Larissa <larry67@xmail.com>   Jul 29, 2014,
to me   7:32 AM

Life is just SO much better when you can buy
stuff!!! Like really!!!
Poopoo!!!!

....

Eirinie <eirinieeee@xmail.com>   Jul 29, 2014,
to Larissa   9:11 AM

Tellllll me about it!

....

THINGS LONG

SINCE PAST

We were poor for the duration of our friendship. We really never had much, even when I would get the occasional lucrative job. Neither of us was good at saving, we preferred fleeting moments of joy and splendor, particularly you. We would get champagne, or takeout, or take a cab even though we knew that twenty quid would be the difference between making rent on time and not in about three weeks. We couldn't hold on to it. I couldn't hold on to it.

It was way more fun to go out, buy a dress, revel in the material shit rather than save for a future neither of us could imagine. At the end of the month, we would usually have nothing in the fridge but some too-old takeout and maybe something you had made, leftovers that some would argue were too small a portion to bother keeping, but you never threw anything out.

A meal for us was often just a potato, one sad potato with whatever rind of cheese was left, maybe some frozen sweet corn, salt and butter if we had it. I would make you a potato, you would make me a potato, we preferred them baked but rarely had the patience and so boiled and then fried was often the way. I almost salivate at the memory. Isn't that funny? A meal that, at the time, was not memorable or special in the slightest is now something that catapults me back to our East Finchley flat, a cold day maybe, huddled under blankets because we were too cheap and too poor to have the heating on, warming ourselves on too-hot potatoes.

You in the kitchen, silently making food, hair wrapped, those faux-Adidas two-stripe sweatpants on, a man's dress shirt. You might turn, ask if I want some, a small gesture that might be lost on anyone else, but I knew, I knew how much love it contained. If you didn't love me you wouldn't have offered, you'd make your food and go watch *Everwood* or *Grey's Anatomy* or some other shit and ignore me entirely. Your love was such a quiet thing some-times, but I had never been so certain that someone loved me before. Your mood fluctuated, yes, but you were steady in your regard for me. Your silence didn't chill me like it did so many other people, I didn't fret that you hated me when you closed your bed-room door and had wine in your room by yourself. I knew you; I knew your need for solitude. I also knew that the moment you needed me you would fling open the door and ask what I was do-ing, maybe get in bed next to me or give me a hug from behind whilst I did the washing up (you loved when I did the washing up, or any household chore to be honest).

We could go out together to a bar, I could be having a blast but you would want to go home and so you would, heading out in a cab you couldn't afford, but I knew this had nothing to do with me. I knew I was free to party; I knew there was no other meaning to your departure.

Larissa <larry67@xmail.com>   Jun 8, 2014,
to me   4:08 AM

We've moved house again I live 5mins
walking distance from bea now more
central. It's great I'm walking distance
from everything, Montmartre, pigalle, the
louvre, opera, etc etc it's smaller than
the last place but more charming and very
cute there's a little courtyard and it's
kind of loft style
Wish you'll see one day!!

Eirinie <eirinieeee@xmail.com>   Jun 12, 2014,
to Larissa   1:11 AM

Poo poo head!

How come you moved houses again? Did you
not like the last one?
Adam and I are in England for Christmas
this year, are you? We are having NYE
dinner in London with Jamie, Samantha etc
if you are?

How's Beatrice? Do you still love Paris?
Do you think you'll stay forever?

X

PARIS

I feel like a too-full glass of water. I get off the plane and into the cab somehow, even with my secondary school French skills, and I've sort of kept my cool. I feel like I am keeping it all buttoned down, a stuffed shirt, for some reason trying to keep a lid on my feelings, save them for two days' time when I will be burying your body.

I arrive at the Airbnb a full day before our friend Charlie and once inside, once I shed my coat and my bags and wash the plane off my body and brush my teeth, I look out the window onto Paris. I hear people talking in the streets, the clink of wineglasses at cafes, I see the light that is like no other light on Earth hit the buildings and I think to myself, this is why you loved it.

I have never been a huge fan of Paris. It is a beautiful iconic city, but the people there have never endeared themselves to me. I have never had the inclination to live there, even when I would visit you and see your life, it never filled me with longing. Now, as I wander out onto the street to covertly follow my Google Maps to the nearest bar, my heart swells with desire. The city you loved so much is now synonymous with you. I mean, there are so many places that will (much later) trigger me—New York, that one pub in Camden, West London casting studios, Enfield . . . but this is different. I had a French boyfriend once upon a time and when he found out you moved to Paris he said, "Larissa was Parisienne before she ever moved there." Now I understand completely what he meant. So much of this city is you. The style, the brightness, the classic beauty, the secret seediness. Every corner my phone tells me to turn and I dutifully do, I expect to see you. I wouldn't even be surprised; it wouldn't be shocking. Just being here feels like I have uttered the magic words and so much of you has come back to me, to see you here would simply be the final stage of the incantation. I probably wouldn't even hug you; we would probably just smile at each other without saying words, walk to the bar together, sink a glass of your favourite merlot before you dissipated back into the city walls.

But you don't show yourself. It's almost a tease because I feel you everywhere and I feel insane for thinking that but there is just so much of you here. When I was in LA and had found out you were dead I felt so distant, so jealous of your French friends that they could be together like a conjuring circle, holding hands and feeling the table move. And now I am here I know I was right to be jealous because here you fucking are, the closest you could be to me. The table is moving and the Ouija board is flickering.

At the bar I meet Natalia, one of your oldest friends. We hug the sort of hug that says so much without uttering a word and before I know it I am rocking her side to side as I hug her, light on my feet. This is a patented Larissa move, this rocking, and Natalia seems to sense it as she pulls back to say "Eirins," just as you would have. There is so much we have to say to each other but we sit at the bar in silence for a moment, strangled by the noose of our own words. When we have cried and drunk and hugged some more it is late and I need to be in the outskirts of Paris in the morning to see your mother and your aunt. We part ways and on my short walk home, between my sorrow and my drunkenness, I could swear you are somewhere out of eyesight, somewhere just in the shadows.

The next day I wake reluctantly. I don't want to go and see your mum. I don't want to see her agony. A few weeks ago, when Charlie asked if I wanted her to come and be with me in Paris I jumped at it feverishly. I wanted that so badly, I couldn't imagine wanting to be alone with the specters of your city, but now, when she arrives, I resent her for it. As if she is intruding. It isn't fair at all, or logical, so I brush those feelings aside. It is short-lived, because once we are on the long train ride to your aunt's house, I hold her hand and am so grateful I don't have to make this most dreaded journey alone. We get there, meet Natalia, head into your aunt's council flat. It is in an area of Paris I have never been to, mostly Black and brown faces, no glitz or glamour here, just people trying to live. Inside your aunt's flat I see you, wide, catlike eyes, slight frame perched regally on the edge of the sofa. I hesitate, for a split second I think I am going mad but then it clicks and I remember who I am here to visit. You always were the spitting image of your mum down to the details: the bones in your hands felt like holding a bird in mine, delicate and fragile, her smell your smell. We hug and she can scarcely keep it together.

When we sit your mother is still sobbing as she asks me what I know. I know nothing. I know the party line, it was an accident in the bath, I am sticking to this because anything else feels too close to destruction. Instead, I reminisce, it is all I have brought with me, my memories. I realise too late that flowers or chocolates or some sweet token would have been appropriate, but instead I offer your mum stories of you. I cherry-pick, little decadent truffles from my mind, stories of you in your best light. I do not speak of our conversations in the last few months, your broken heart post-breakup, your aimlessness, your worry that your life wouldn't move on. I tell her of your lavish taste, the times we missed buses and had to wait, huddled for a night bus forty minutes out. The jokes, the warmth of the flats we shared. Your mum can barely contain her bittersweet happiness, even when I run out of things to say she is still on the edge of her seat wanting more.

We all sob hard at your funeral. Cling to each other like the ship-wrecked, wetting each other's dress collars with tears, despite not having seen each other in days and months and years. It's funny what extreme happiness or sadness can do to a person. Makes you exposed, raw, ready to share that thing that you promised your-self you'd never tell anybody. Maddy and Natalia and Simon and Antoni, your ex Pierre, all of us lost without you, struggling to make it through the service.

The church is beautiful, Parisian to the core, old and preserved. Right in the heart of the city. We all eat and drink before the service, needing fortification, needing to feel the warmth of our group, thrown together for the first time in many a moon for this, the blackest of occasions. We drink, we keep things light. I cannot face eating, although urged by many to do so. My stomach will not allow solids, a constant churn of nausea keeps me from the plates of Middle Eastern foods everyone is sharing. I constantly check my pockets for the words I have written for you, about you. I need my script, without it I will be afloat on my grief, struggling to keep my head up. I need it.

The priest is a Catholic, my worst denomination. He says so many things about sins and the sinner that make me snort out loud, furious with him, furious with everyone who has allowed him to be there. How dare he question what kind of life you led? How dare he tiptoe around the possibility of you being in heaven, whatever that may be? How dare he do anything other than summon platitudes and quiet reflection, this sorcerer, this phony, this mortal man who did not know you?

It isn't the last thing he does that makes me question the necessity of his presence. We are running behind schedule, people were late and busy talking and consoling and doing the things people do at funerals. The priest ushers us to our seats, suggests whoever needs to speak about you do so quickly. I feel rushed but I take my place at the lectern, hurry my words, and then, as planned, I play a voice note you had sent Maddy and me, one of your trademark cackle laughing at some joke Maddy had told. It was a two-minute voice note, and even when I listen to it now I can feel something crack within me, leaving me halved. One half laughing with you, the other tearing with sorrow that this is all I have left of that magnificent cackle. I play it in that church and it echoes, as sounds in old churches are wont to do. I hold my breath waiting for a response, scared I have cracked that room in two, too. But people laugh with you. I smile. We all smile through the tears. It is impossible to hear your laugh and not smile.

I'm not certain how I get to the cemetery. I know it is in Pierre's vintage car, from which (in between some of the most French road rage I have ever seen) he gives us bite-size chunks of a guided tour of Paris. He talks about the light, how Paris is known as the City of Lights not because of the twinkling of electricity that can be viewed from Montmartre, but because the city has height restrictions and buildings are not permitted to be above a certain story, meaning that natural light pours in ways unheard-of in other cities. As he speaks I can see curtains of sunrays, the air in motion in the light. Before I know it, we are at a graveyard, vast and gated and segmented.

We drive in for a good few minutes before finding the plot. My heart sinks when I see how crowded it is, scarcely room for all of us to stand without desecrating someone else's resting place. I feel disconnected at this point, I don't want to be here. I want this part to be over, I don't want to stand by your grave, by what's left of your body in a fucking box. It feels macabre, it doesn't feel like we're honouring you. "She's not even here!" I want to scream at everyone. Because you're not, there is no sense of this being anything other than a dump site but I rebuke this thought in my head, thinking of what is appropriate. We should be here. This is what people do.

I am desperate to be anywhere else. Natalia sings something, it's pretty but it's deeply God-ish and I am not in the mood for the promise of a saviour. Dean, your old modelling agent (and mine, come to think of it), goes to the grave, begins shoveling dirt in as no one else seems capable. We take it in turns, a heaping of dirt. I can't remember if I shovel too, but I remember having a hard time breathing, people feel too close, I need space.

The grave fills. I am very aware of your mum, who cannot seem to stand for long, her legs seem to give out from under her as if her body is saying that's enough, no more, we can't. I want to help her, to hold her, but her Ghanaian family surrounds her, each holding an arm or an elbow or steadying her with a palm at her back. I briefly wonder if they would do the same for me, were I to go over to them.

Darkness comes quickly, I had no idea it was so late and now Pierre's car is filled with people heading to your aunt's house for a formal wake. I don't want to go; I cannot keep myself buttoned-up any longer. I need to drink and laugh about you. I cannot watch your mum cry anymore and so I tell him I will meet him at the bar where some of her less familiar friends are gathering. I can't tell if he's disappointed and I don't really care.

The bar is small, your friends tell me it was your favourite. I have cobbled together, thinking of it only at the last moment, a playlist of your favourite songs on Spotify and I put it on. It's such a hodge-podge because you liked so many things—the Doors, Mobb Deep, that Lil' Kim song you knew all the words to, the Brian Jonestown Massacre, Elliott Smith. It's quite jarring, this mix, I understand why the friends who are present who did not know you as well as Pierre and Maddy and Jen and I are not vibing with it. It keeps being turned off for some generic French house music and I am fuming, I had a plan for this evening, a plan to evoke your spirit, to make it feel like we were listening to your tinny speakers you had shoved into your aging laptop whilst you smoked out the window and poured wine for the night ahead. I want to be with the people you knew, I want to tell stories about you, I want to laugh and cry and whatever else is necessary to feel like I really have a hold on you. But the music is too loud, you wouldn't have liked this shit, this driving beat with no lyrics and no discernable soul.

The party moves to Simon's place but again it begins to feel as if people don't want to talk about you. I am drunk now, I ask some of your friends (the ones I don't know and therefore share none of your history with) for anecdotes, anything really. I feel like your mum on the day I showed up, desperate and eager and parched for the lack of you. Eventually I decide this is fruitless, this is fishing, this is so painful I want to be on my own. Pierre offers to walk me back and I accept, feeling out of my depth in this city all of a sudden, I am lost and I want to be home.

The city is still, definitely more still than London would be at this hour, although what hour it is I am not sure. We walk for a while in a silence punctuated with banal little comments about how lovely the service was, how beautiful the church. Pierre stops and turns to me, says there's so much she would want you to know, I have so much to tell you and not enough time. It feels like fate, I almost want to hold his hand in a moment of solidarity, I am finally going to get my wish but now I feel sick with the possibility of what he might say.

As we wind closer to my place in the seventeenth arrondissement, Pierre tells me many of your secrets. They spill out of him and I wonder how long he has been waiting, how painful this day must have been for him. Some things I know already, I know you were lonely, I know you were broke and heartbroken. Some things I do not. Some things catch in my throat but I don't want to stop the steady stream coming from Pierre, I try to take them in my stride.

He speaks with such candor about your moods, with intricacy about the time directly prior to your death that I begin to think how much better he knew you than I; of course I knew you but a thing I have been mulling over is: Did I know you at the end? Maybe this long and storied history of you and I is not enough? I should have known more. I should have done more.

I didn't fully appreciate how sad you were, Larissa. I didn't realise how you said the water in your new apartment tasted weird, how you had bought bottled because you didn't want to drink the tap, how you died in that water.

By the time Pierre grips my hand at the door of my apartment, kisses my cheeks the way the French do, I feel completely sober and so full of you, not completely in a good way. I need to lie down. Charlie is already asleep inside, I slip in under the white linen sheet, I slip in beside her, wide awake and wanting to go home.

Larissa <larry67@xmail.com>   Nov 21, 2009,
to me   2:32 AM

So if you tell me what you want for lunch
ill make sure I got the ingredients at
home ;) I'm thinking light and healthy
like veg and stuff but I will make a cake
of some sort!! then we can settle down for
a glass (bottle) of vino!!

We have to get you out of your rut and
into the world so I'm adamant that we do
this and do it right!
Loves you xxxx

—

Sent from my mobile device

FINDING A THERAPIST

I t's been two weeks but feels simultaneously like two years and two minutes. I cannot get a grip on my pain; it seems to spiral out of my hands every time I try to rein it in. I sob, loudly, in my acting class. I scream at my husband, as petulant as a teen, telling him he doesn't understand, telling him if his best friend died I would never ask him to continue performing mundanities to keep the household ticking over. I am livid and frenzied and desperately sad.

My dear friends suggest a grief therapist, something I had been pondering but had dismissed as a luxury. At their behest I visit my doctor and, true to my current form, I sob uncontrollably in his office. And, true to an American doctor's form, he swiftly writes me a prescription for Xanax that I take even though I think it's overkill. He also suggests Blue Lake Therapy, and when I get home I take to the internet, staring at the faces and the blurbs of therapists who seem to promise hope and solace and understanding. I try to imprint on one of these white, friendly faces, because they are all white. Do I want a man? A father figure? A young woman, a peer? What about a woman my mother's age? I know that I have an ease when talking with men, a familiarity I view as kinship but upon closer inspection looks more like deference. A nagging feeling pulls at my chest as I book an appointment with Tom, a bespectacled older man, balding and kind-faced.

When the appointment date comes around, I am desperate for therapy. Desperate to vomit up all the words and thoughts and feelings I have been swallowing in my daily life in order to not scare my child or the cashier at Whole Foods. I sit in the waiting room, which is all warm neutrals and cacti and soft lighting, and I am filled with optimism. An improbable ocean comes in over the speakers, lapping waves on sand. This is what I needed. Yes. The walls seem thin, flimsy, and for a fleeting moment I am worried that someone will hear all the secrets I have for my therapist's ears.

Tom ushers me into his office, equally warm with its whites and cacti and generic bold prints framed simply in black. I sit on a midcentury chair, I recognise it from some hip furniture company that is always bombarding my Instagram feed. It isn't very comfortable—my first sign that this will not be a pleasant experience. I begin by giving a brief outline of what I consider to be the most pertinent information: my best friend died a few weeks ago, it was sudden, it is under investigation, I feel adrift. I think I describe Larissa as "rock and roll," I mention the Ramones maybe, and before I know it Tom is filling me in on his history with rock and roll. Now I know he was at CBGB in the eighties, now I know he was once in a band. It's jarring, this personal history. I falter in my tracks, which leaves a Tom-sized gap for him to slide into.

He begins to talk about what solitude and reflection look like—for him, it's his house in Joshua Tree. He and his wife bought it a few years back with the intention of retiring there but now they spend most weekends visiting it, doing it up little by little. Under ordinary circumstances I would love to know about his house in Joshua Tree, I would love to know where he was thrifting the antiques, what paint colours he was going for, would love to weigh in on pool versus hot tub. But right now, I feel robbed. His speech is peppered with a lot of inspirational poster–like slogans, trite little sentences on grief that are easily googled, easily said, empty platitudes and words of hope. I keep trying to assert myself and it takes all of my energy to bring it back to Larissa, back to me. I am a person who often makes a lot of room for others in my conversations with little space for me, and I recognise this pattern repeating here in this room in which I am supposed to be so unguarded.

Suddenly Tom is asking about drugs, did she take drugs and what kind and I am so blindsided I stammer and then the hour is up. The hour is up and I know absolutely everything about Tom and his marriage but am pretty solidly sure he could not even correctly pronounce my name if prompted. I am supposed to provide my credit card now and as he lines up the Square for me to pay, I feel cheated. What the fuck was that? Was that therapy? I don't feel better, I feel angrier. I have a twenty-minute walk home and I cry the whole way, grateful that it is dark out and the streetlights sporadic.

It takes me a full week to brave the Blue Lake Therapy website again. Adam mentions it a couple of times, timidly, and I shoot him down every time. One hundred dollars to listen to someone else talk? Fuck that. You can get that for free at the checkout line of Trader Joe's. What I know now does not even occur to me—that finding a great therapist is much like finding a best friend as an adult: harrowing, long, and seemingly impossible. But like finding grown-up mates, the payoff is so much bigger when you eventually, finally find The One.

Julie is right there on the Blue Lake Therapy website, just beneath Tom and his Joshua Tree retirement plan. She is older, probably my mum's age, stylish in a sort of Nancy Meyers way. Her bio explicitly states her solidarity with the Black community and I think, fine Julie, fine. I'll go, I'll go, I'll go, I'll go, I'll go. Adam can scarcely contain his joy that I am going back. He presses the family credit card into my hand as I leave.

When I get there, she is kind and competent, giving off a distinct intellectual vibe. She is smart and concise; she listens with not only interest but comprehension. Julie also has a musician husband, also has a biracial daughter. And we click, really click in a way that seems the utter antithesis of me and Tom, it makes me wonder how many more Toms I could have encountered before finding my Julie. No wonder so many of my friends have been completely turned off by the experience of looking for a therapist, it is so utterly disheartening to spend an entire hour giving a broad overview of my problems and life and circumstance only to realise at the end of that hour that it was an utterly pointless expulsion of energy. To drag oneself to yet another doctor for yet another recommendation in the seemingly futile hope of finding someone who gels with you, not to mention the financial drain of this cycle, is so depleting that a couple of cocktails seem way more cost-effective and immediate.

Julie sees me through some of the toughest parts of my grieving process. The trepidation of the funeral, the verdict on cause of death, the guilt of days spent feeling good and then remembering I should be sad, Julie is there throughout. It is such a relief to have someone impartial listen to your issues, to gently paw through your many grievances with care and intelligence and insight. Sometimes I voice something I have been mulling over in my head for a while or even something I know to be true since birth and just voicing it out loud to Julie is enough for it to take on a different meaning altogether, changing my knowledge of self and my origin story irrevocably.

I am not good at talking about myself for an extended period of time, it feels self-indulgent and gratuitous to me, but with Julie it is permissible, preferable even. She only mentions herself and her life within the context of providing a greater understanding of a subject. To this day I still don't know what her retirement plans are.

```
    me:  larry?                                    10:16 AM
         you there?
Larissa:  yarr
         wats up?
    me:  why havent you left yet
         we have to jet soon!

Larissa:  jet where?!!                             10:17 AM
    me:  into the city for food?~?~!?!?!
         then to this guys terrace
         i told holly and emailed you!
Larissa:  o ok
    me:  are you ready to leave??? coz you
         have about 25 mins to get here
Larissa:  yeh just read the message
         o jeez
         ummm
         ok

         ill get ready then                        10:18 AM
         i didnt realise had to b there soon
    me:  yes! duh!
Larissa:  i was chillaxing
    me:  its like almost 2 im bored
         wanna go do stuff
Larissa:  ok
    me:  eric was planning stuff for us to do
         so wanted you to be in on it!
         is holly ready??

         also whats the yank no?                   10:19 AM


         does the silence mean youve left?         10:23 AM


Larissa:  yes                                      10:24 AM
         we are in a cab now
    me:  ha
         lies
         lies
Larissa:  on my laptop!
         lols
```

```
       me:  HAHAHAHA are you?                        10:24 AM
  Larissa:  soon! just getting ready!
            2 mins
       me:  oh gee whizz. i know your 2 mins
            its like, 10 mins
  Larissa:  5!
       me:  im bored and lonely
            and i love how the number is
            escalating
  Larissa:  dude me typing means im not getting     10:25 AM
            ready
       me:  sorry
            shhhh
            bye
  Larissa:  lol
            ok bye!!÷
```

C H A P T E R   5

A YEAR LATER

I t's almost been a year. A whole year without you. I should call your mum, or write to her. I have a draft in my docs that I started and never finished marked "Larissa's mum" but I didn't know what to say to someone whose grief and pain and trauma are unfathomable to all, even me.

I miss you terribly. Not all the time as I was expecting, but often, apropos of nothing, I am devastated all over again. Trying to remember the details of a story only you and I were privy to and thinking to call you and realising suddenly that I can't. These stories are now mine to remember, the burden of our history, long but simple as it was, falls on my shoulders. I don't want it. I don't want to remember our trips to New York on my own. I don't want to think about that bar, Clem's, that probably still exists but is definitely different, out in Brooklyn where we drank underage and marveled at the size of the shots. I don't want to remember that man, that old Black man in his designated seat at the bar who, when you walked into the room, said, "Damn girl, you look like a Tutankhamen exhibit," and we laughed so hard he turned away from us. I don't want to think about these things alone. They are ours, not just mine. What if I forget? Or misremember? Now I come to think of it, was he even that old? Did he turn away or is that a fabrication of a storyteller's mind?

Remember when we used to go to the Collection? What a weird, weird old place that was. Had the vibe of a venue that was once very hip in the nineties, right on Brompton Road in West London. A large, polished warehouse space, private tables, expensive mediocre food, a bar with prices that would take your breath away. I went there once and met the owner, knew he would love you, brought you down one night dressed in our finery (where did you get that Cavalli dress?), and we paid for nothing, which was good because we were broke.

It was very much our routine, when absolutely stone-cold poor, to get dressed in the best things we owned, go out and share a wine until some poor chump bought us a bottle, two. Never got so much as a handshake from us, not so much as a smile from you (unless he was an intellectual or a rock star), but some nights that was the only thing we ate or drank. We named them, all those strangers left behind at bars as we giggled our way home for our own after-party, we called them our sponsors.

But that Cavalli dress. God, that dress. Sheer, meant to be worn with nothing beneath, but despite your rock and roll heart you were modest to the point of conservatism and so you always wore it with a slip. You were breathtaking. It took you an absolute age to get dressed to go out; at the time we needed to leave you were just begrudgingly getting in the shower. I would be done, two glasses of cheap merlot in, dressed to the nines and whining at you to hurry, but I have never known you to hurry. Once you were a full day late to a *Dazed and Confused* shoot.

You would take hours to get ready, and even then, with the cab honking at the door, you moved like the twenty-four-hour day meant nothing to you. Truly you had no use for time, it took as long as it took and when you were over it, you were gone. Later, when we had a little more money and would occasionally go to dinner, I knew to ask for the cheque along with our last cocktail, so that the second we were done we could get up and leave, no hesitation. That was your least favourite thing, antsily waiting for a bill to be paid or someone to gather their things when you had been ready to go. Ironic given your own personal scheduling. Sometimes you would say "I'll wait outside, here's some money" just to get out of the door. It drove you crazy to be somewhere when you were done with it.

It's one of the reasons Maddy and I once pondered if it was maybe your time to go. Don't get me wrong, every single god-damn day I resent that you are not here. But you were peculiar that way. You knew how to make an entrance, knew when to exit. You died beautiful, which I know you would have appreciated.

Where are you?

There was a day in LA. That awful day when Natalia called me and I knew before she finished her sentence what she was trying to tell me, through tears. Prostrate and breathless on the bed as Adam tried to understand, tried to make me tell him what was wrong before he too could not bear to hear it uttered. That day, I stood outside on the front step, my grief facing the street and all of the passing cars. A butterfly came out of nowhere and would not leave my side. Was that you? I like to think it was you but also, if you were to return to me as anything, I don't think a white butterfly would be the thing. I think you would choose something funny, a persistent wasp, the low hum of an amp forever in my ears, the taste of your favourite wine in everything I drank. Poetic that way. Definitely not a cat, despite your feline face. You hated them and they loved you. Like most people who met you.

I wonder what I should tell your mother. That woman who looks so much like you that at your funeral I could not so much as steal a glance at her. The woman who, as I watched her from the corner of my eye break down from the sorrow, made my heart empty out as I realised my sadness was nothing to hers. What can I tell her? What can I give her?

I now know, now that you're gone, how much you compartmentalised your friends and family. Very few of us were witness to your whole truth, and I still am not sure if that was a means of self-preservation, or to keep us safe. And your mum got to see so little of your complexities, like all our mums, I suppose. We don't let them see all of the truths, ugly as they may be, don't want them to be disappointed, or angry, or even just surprised. Most of us still just want to make our mums proud and if my mum knew half the things we had done, Larissa, I cannot imagine her swelling with pride.

Perhaps what I can give your mother is a little of your truth. Not too much, don't worry. Just enough to show her some of that fullness, to let her know how much we all loved you, how rich you made my life and so many others', how you are missed.

I will tell her about all of the cool, air-conditioned bars we went to in New York when the humidity was too much for us. What a stir we caused, all those long, brown limbs, those estuary accents, improbable and delightful. The times we went to clubs where I would dance and you would watch from the sidelines, drinking and laughing at me, refusing to join. The times in London when I would be working late at a bar and you would call and ask me to come home, and when I did you would have a bottle of something and we would talk into the night, and then not talk at all the next morning, having said all we had to say.

I will tell her how comfortable I was in your trademark silences, the ones that made so many people nervous. How I knew what they meant and just how to treat them. How you told me that I might be one of the few people who really knew you, even though I'm sure I was not the only person you said that to.

I will tell her about the meals we had, the times when you were broke and I paid, or I was broke and you paid, never tallying scores up to hold over the other's head at a later date. I will tell her about the fluidity of our relationship, the ease with which we could be around each other, things unspoken but known.

About our DJ night, the one we made flyers for that was going to be called something Noir, or Noir something (see? If you were still here, I could text you and ask you). The one we abandoned when we realised we didn't know how to use any of the DJ programmes and didn't care enough to learn.

About all those nights we snuck out to White Heat or After School (or was it Skool? Answer me that, Larissa) or Trash and took countless night buses back to Enfield, to creep up those stairs to your room without waking your mum.

About how you would sometimes come back with a dress you found in a vintage shop that you thought would look good on me and you were always right.

I will tell her that I like to imagine you at the sidelines watching me, as if I am dancing alone, only confident because I know you are there.

I will tell your mum these things because she should know what her daughter meant to a girl who never felt cool, still doesn't feel cool, unless she is standing next to you.

I will say, "Your daughter was the best friend I could have asked for at a period of life when I needed her most, and I hope that means something to you because it means absolutely everything to me."

Eirinie <eirinieeee@xmail.com >   Nov 5, 2013,
to Larissa   10:29 AM

Poo poo face,
How exciting! Jesus if this gets to be
your job forever I will be so jealous, is
there anything more rewarding than your
passion being your job?!
When is the launch?
By organise a shoot I meant to get some
photos of my nips, forgetting that I have
about A MILLION ON FILE! Someone def needs
to do something with the one lens took!
It's too awesome not to.

Ps I'm going to start writing again, you
know I haven't for like two years?!?!?!
I'm just going to quietly put things on a
blog until I'm ready for submissions
etc . . . I need to do something more than
just modelling because I feel empty!

Xxx

—

Sent from my iPad

Larissa <larry67@xmail.com>   Nov 5, 2013,
to me   10:51 AM

I know i havent read a book in 2years
either.
Well i need to make a living for myself
and i def cant rely on modeling - so im
jealous of YOU!
good to start writing
launch in Jan. thats when im gonna print
the mag - first print run 1,500! woohoo.
if you can get it in some shops in San
Fran that would be cool. Obvs im gona give
it to City Lights. Maybe i can send you my
████ nterview to read and critic and edit
cause i cant get any objectivity i need
someone to llok at it. its first draft so
dont be too brutal and the layout is a
work in progress - im trying out different
fonts and quote boxes etc so just need
opinion on text
thanks poo head
xxx

CHAPTER 6

CREATION

I started writing as a child. I was eleven when I wrote my first "novel"—really I just filled a purple notebook I got for Christmas with my large scrawl, clumsily plagiarizing Jane Austen. I titled it "Relative Blunders." Its original title, "Family Mistakes," seemed too pedestrian, too simple, and so I opened my thesaurus (which I also got for Christmas that year) and arrived at "Relative Blunders."

My mum loved (still loves) to parade that little tidbit of information around. She always thought I could do more with my brain, focus more on my writing and school than I did on my modelling career. This was a source of great amusement to me and you, Larissa, as your mum thought you spent too much time with your head in books, should care more about the castings and shoots you were missing than the ramblings of long-dead French poets. We would joke that we should swap mums because no doubt you could have made my mum happier than I made her, and vice versa.

I wrote a bit when we were living together, on a barely functioning ancient MacBook that was salvaged from a relationship in
a similar state. When I wrote I would offer you the fragmented
stories, timidly, because I knew the heavy tomes you buried your
head in: Nabokov, Cocteau, Voltaire. You were always kind but
heavy with the editing pen. You wanted my writing to be more
form, less function. You would edit out swathes of text dedicated
to the logistics of a scene perhaps, the nitty-gritty of getting from
A to B, and leave only the flowery, the ornate. My writing became curlicues and decorative fleurs-de-lis under your tutelage. I
so desperately wanted you to think I was smart and worthy and
interesting.

You were one of those people who when you shined your light
on someone everyone else immediately thought they were important and worthy, too. A skill impossible to re-create or imitate, this
bright spotlight of yours incurred a transformation, and I was no
different. Suddenly I was the rock 'n' roll babe I'd dreamed of being, suddenly my leather jacket was authentic, suddenly I smoked,
suddenly men treated me like a goddess, a force to be reckoned
with. Would I have been this person without you? Would I have
been bold and fearless without you by my side, provoking me
and laughing with joy when I succeeded at anything? I will never
know, you were with me throughout my most formative years,
you are so intrinsically linked to my molding that I cannot think
about my fundamental traits (my laughter, what I am told is my
sexiness, my taste in books and music, fuck, even my walk when
in heels) without also thinking of you.

....

Larissa <larry67@xmail.com>   May 25, 2009,
to me   3:20 AM

sorry i missed your call babes
what went down last night then? tell me
everything!

Ill be in all day, mum gies away wed so
party on weekend?!

hope your ok x x x

....

62 BROADFIELD ROAD

62 Broadfield Road is a normal row house in Enfield, northeast London. Pretty nondescript; even after spending copious amounts of time and briefly living there, I will still on occasion pass right by it. Downstairs was clean and familial, photos of you and your brother, or you and your brother and your mother posed and smiling. The kitchen with the slow cooker on the counter, the laundry drying on the rack by the back door. Occasional reminders of Christ, a crucifix or a verse of scripture. I haven't been back to that house in about three years; the images I summon of it are hazy but these are the things I remember about your mother's home.

It wasn't flashy and truly I don't think anything changed during the fifteen-odd years I visited the house. The wallpaper remained the same, that one railing on the banister was always broken, the kitchen always smelled like your mum's cooking. There was something so soothing about the sameness. My family moved a lot when I was a kid, finally settling when I was fifteen in a small Scottish border town that I despised, and the consistency of your mother's home was what made it feel so safe to me, I think.

And then, up the stairs, your brother's small box of a room, to the left the bathroom, then left again your room, and finally your mother's. Eventually the attic was renovated into a bedroom and it became yours, and a trademark of visiting you was creeping up those creaky-ass stairs at three in the morning, hoping your mum wouldn't hear below (I still cannot believe that we were never chastised or questioned about our nighttime wanderings, but perhaps your mum was a very deep sleeper). But back then opening the door to your room was mind-blowing to me, at least when I first visited as a teen. My room at home was basic, the same tear-outs from *Kerrang!* magazine, the same *Simpsons* posters. Typical, unoriginal. Yours . . . yours featured pinups I simply had never thought of, a row of Kate Moss Rimmel ads pulled out of fashion magazines, poems printed out and tacked up, black-and-white photos of jazz musicians and Charlie Chaplin. The eyes of the Misfits, Sid and Nancy stared moodily back at me in torn tights and oversized T-shirts and slept-in hair. Not the typical sixteen-year-old bedroom décor, not in my experience. Cooler than everyone even then.

Eventually, when I became comfortable at my then modelling agency Storm, I stole you a Kate Moss comp card. They repped her and when I handed you the card, you stared at it and read the measurements and looked at the photos and I knew it was a good gift, a thought that was cemented when you stuck it up beside your other Kates, pride of place on your wall.

I was mostly a good girl then, and still have the tendency to want to abide by the rules, be patted on the head by the adults, and so when you introduced me to the scene you were in, all those clubs and nights and older boys, I was nervous. I didn't dress right. I had never danced to music in public before, not in a venue that wasn't a family wedding or school disco, two events that left me sorely unqualified to step out on the floor of White Heat and pout my way through a Depeche Mode song. I went with you, scared and dressed in my best outfits, probably a minidress or denim cut-off skirt and a borrowed shirt, ripped tights at your instruction, too much eyeliner.

I learnt many things on those nights, I learnt what it felt like to be surrounded by boys I found attractive instead of the five-foot-nothing boys of my class at school (I was five foot ten inches and growing), I learnt what it felt like to know, truly fucking know I was cool because I was with you, in your crew. People knew you, shouted your name across the bar, and then, in a bid to please you, learnt my name too, smiled into my face. You commanded respect as a sixteen-year-old and I was in awe. We would dance, or I would, you would flirt with some skinny white boy who was pale to the point of incandescence, we would maybe get two drinks bought for us, share them, setting in stone a pattern that was to be ours for a lifetime. Your lifetime.

Finally, the lights would flicker on, closing time. We would traipse out into the cold London air, stand at a night bus stand for twenty-five minutes, do the same at the second bus station. It would take us literal hours to get to your house in Enfield but it never crossed my mind to ponder if it was worth the three-hour round trip for an equal amount of time dancing to Test Icicles. It seemed worth it, it was something of an education for me, my introduction to a scene, the characters of which I would be seeing around for a long time. Some of whom I still speak to today.

What would you wear? What was your style back then? Always black, maybe a red scarf in your hair tied around your crown, hair pulled back in a high dancer's bun. Winged eyeliner, your time-less signature. Tight, tiny jeans, ripped at the knees. Harness biker boots. I think there was a time you wore a bandana around your wrist, although I can't recall exactly when. Were there photogra-phers at After School and Trash and White Heat? Those annoying ones who ignore you when you look your best but whose lenses somehow find you at the end of the night when you're tired and disheveled. If there were, my god what a treasure trove they must be sitting on. I would love to see those times, those outfits, those faces of Dev and Matty and Wade and Jenny and Pete and Joe.

I do remember a photo book coming out a few years later, a very early 2000s theme—the photographer would take a quick snap of someone, catch them unawares, and then get them to pose for another. The book was a side-by-side of various people we knew, were you in it? Does that book still exist somewhere, wait-ing to be unearthed in a box of your things at 62 Broadfield Road?

I remember having so much fun then, I think I probably danced too much during a time when absolutely no one danced, it was cooler to lean against the walls and pretend whatever song made you feel dead inside, but I remember the fun. I also remember how nervous I was, like all fifteen-year-olds I worried I was doing it wrong, I tried to take on the affectation everyone else seemed to have, bored and unfazed, but I was dazzled. It was what I had been looking for, it was nothing like the kids at school, it was nothing like having to pretend I liked the shit those people liked, it was like finding my habitat. You opened that door for me, you made that possible. You created space within me to be someone different, I didn't have to follow, I didn't have to colour within the lines. This was liberation.

I wonder if anyone else from those days felt that way about that scene. I wonder whether moving away from London to someplace with nothing cool about it made me exceedingly grateful to have this little enclave to cling to. Was it as great as I remember? Like the night Amy Winehouse came to After School, was she with Nick Grimshaw or something? It was the early, early Winehouse days, pre–pinup girl look. Or the night a supermodel came, and you and I were giddy with excitement.

And after all that, after all the thrills and the light buzz from whatever cheap vodka we drank, we would lean on each other's shoulders on the top of the night bus, sleepy and cold, illuminated to the dark world outside the windows, until we finally got back to Enfield, back to your mum's still and silent house, back to your bed.

Larissa <larry67@xmail.com>   Jun 25, 2009,
to me   3:20 AM

u bitch im soooooooo listening to
steely dan and LOVING it!!! x x x x

Larissa <larry67@xmail.com>   Jun 25, 2009,
to me   4:50 AM

im STILL listening to dirty work! JEEEEZ O

ok so told mum to cal aunt valerie today
she said shed do it in evening but she
just cleared out the spare bedroom so im
assuming shes expecting her sooner than i
think. ill let u know as soon as i do. i
mean we could just do a weekend now and
then save up a bit go back for longer- o
shit u need to work - hmmm too early to
book holiday? for like cple weeks? bearing
in mind i dont fin summer school til 30th
july so we could go after that

gosh we have so many plans! well im glad
they r all with you!! ;) x x x x x

THE MUSIC

There are songs, whole albums even, that are now inextricably linked to you. The first time I ever listened to the Cure was in the flat in Finsbury Park, I remember the front of the CD, star-covered, a deep black-blue sky hung behind Robert Smith's hair. I remember reaching for it, hesitantly, you had told me to put some music on, gestured to your CDs, I felt pricks of sweat begin to form in my armpits, I felt ill-equipped to be tasked with this but I pulled this one, this record out. You barely registered the music, which to me meant victory. I had chosen correctly. I remember the thrill of hearing something I knew was good, that electricity of discovery. I remember wanting to pull the sleeve of the CD out, examine and absorb it, but I felt too sheepish, that felt like too green of a move.

And then the Smiths. My high school music choices had always swung more metal, I had thought, for some reason, that the harder the music I listened to the more I would be taken as legit, as a valid member of whatever alt crowd. I think it had something to do with being Black in a social scene that was predominantly white. I felt that liking the softer, almost poppier sounds would mean something to others, that I didn't belong, that I couldn't hang. But I heard "How Soon Is Now?" for the first time in that same flat and I felt angry I hadn't found it sooner. It felt so like me, so like slipping on a sad little jacket I had been shunning for years, melancholy and heart-tugging. I stumbled upon your music collection accidentally, you allowed me to paw through your shit, borrowing CDs, delving through your eclectic tastes. Mobb Deep, Le Tigre, the Cramps, the Doors, David Bowie, the Deftones.

I often wonder why as a teen I never really delved into my Black identity. I think the light-skinned privilege I possessed made me avoid any deep analysis. I think that I related more to my whiteness because it was known to me, my Blackness was as unknown as my father. I had the vague understandings of that person, of that part of where I came from, but the details felt too painful to press and so I skirted around it, like itching around a scab. I never thought I'd find a way into that part, never really considered it but Larissa was a conduit, and I felt welcomed into a part of life I had thought would forever be distant to me.

And it wasn't contrived or even conscious, I was considered a part of Larissa's family and viewed as Black and so therefore I was ushered into a room in my heart I hadn't been aware of. I could be Black and still like Korn, or Hole, or even Steely Dan. It was a nice change of perspective, one I don't even think I was aware of until much later in our friendship.

Occasionally, as a teen, if I expressed an opinion that was considered Black, there would be some (white) person who would pop up and say, "You're half white as well, remember." It seemed too difficult to tread the line between my two disparate families, I wasn't sure where I was supposed to be, which side of the line I should be erring on. Larissa was a unifier.

Last Night

 Larissa <larry67@xmail.com>
to me

Mar 17, 2011,
7:44 AM

Sooooo

I have to tell you about my night please!!!
WARNING THERE IS SAME NAMMMEEEEEEE
DROOOOPIINGGG!!!!LOL and its about 10 pages
long!!!!! but need to get it out!!!

Anyway, after my shoot I was all make-
upd up so I thought 'I aint gonna waste
this' so called sash who told me he was
busy blah blah which quite deterred me
and I was so close to going home but after
a glass o wine with mads (who decided to
tell me that not only was she was now a
lesbian with a girlfriend but shes also
dropping out of drama school – Dont even
get me started she is actually samantha
jones) Anyway thats when I called jacko
and was like 'right, lets go get a drink
asap'. turns out hes just moved to soho so
we met in soho and went to the curzon for
starting drink.
As we were leaving we bump into Carl Barat
and him and Jacko are like bum chums or
whatevs and He's like 'hey guys, come
and have a drink blah blah. I'm meeting
Lily Allen in groucho in a sec.' So were
like yeh sounds great – yada yar had a
drink then Jackson said he had to go to
his studio to sort out some rehearsal or
something so we went there and bumped
into Wildcat Will. He's just a well known
rocker that went out with someone from ab
fab I think or bananarama or something.
Anyway hes friends with Kate and all that
jazz so hes like 'come to the W guys its
free drinks ALL night long. (literally an
open bar to order whatever you want on all
7 floors and rooms in the hotel) Ive got
guestlist' So (by this point bear in mind

I am actually kinda drunk) we rock up to
W, theres a thousand paps and me and jacko
get walked through the crowd by the owners
of the hotel and papd down the entrance
carpet !!;)
So we hung and drank etc then Wildcat was
like 'O btw, The Clash and The Who are
playing here in one of the smaller rooms
tonight' Pah! Can you believe! They did
a joint set playing ALL their classics
to like a room of 30. Actually one of the
best gigging moments of my life. Actually.
Omg just gettign chills remembering. So
this is where Kate comes into the story,
cause obvs her and Mick Jones are like
bezzy mates. And of course Jacko happens
to be friends with Mick AND Kate and
Joe (agent Provok Joe) and they are all
there in front row talking about how this
perfermance is rock history in the making.
then we strolled back to his on frith
street at stoopid oclock blind drunk and
obvs got DOWNN. It was amaz we had so much
fun and we had a little kissy and cuddle
this morn then I left!!

now im at work writing you this email!!!
hahahahahahah

mooomalates!!!!!!!!

xxx

....

Eirinie <eirinieeee@xmail.com>   Mar 17, 2011,
to Larissa   10:46 AM

OMGGGGGGGG.
OMGGGGGGGGGGGGGGG
OMGGGGGGGGGGGGGGGGGGGGGGGGGGGGGGGG
I ACTUALLY CANNOT TYPE COZ OF JEALOUSY.
MY EARS ARE STILL RINGING WITH THE SOUND
OF ALL THOSE NAMES YOU DROPPED.
fuck.
why wasnt i there????

....

BLACK ROCK
AND ROLL

L arissa was dressed like a punk. Ripped black jeans, black shirt with the sleeves torn off, hair brushed high, a leaning tower above her, defiant and proud. She had on her harness biker boots, was probably smoking. It was the second time I had ever met her and I thought that she was utterly unreal. I'd never seen a Black person dressed that way; I didn't know that we could. This was pre-Google, I had no way of knowing that there might be people who looked like me and dressed like her. Even my sorry fifteen-year-old attempt at being cool and rock and alt was tepid, a pleated miniskirt, knee-high socks, Etnies skate shoes (I did not skate), a hoodie from a generic festival. I looked like a child but Larissa . . . Larissa was something else. Larissa was Grace Jones she was Paul Hudson she was Skin. That day she solidified in my mind what it could mean to be Black and into rock and metal and punk.

The first time I ever met her I was upstairs at the Garage in Camden for my friend Candy's birthday. There was a teen band playing and I knew the boys and had a huge crush on the drummer, perhaps a foreshadowing of my future taste in men. His name was Daz and he had an eyebrow and lip piercing, neither of which I had ever seen on a Black kid my age in real life, and he reminded me of N*E*R*D-era Pharrell Williams with his nonchalance, swagger, and skateboarding. I owned a demo his band, Error, had made that was full of songs with lofty, meaningless names like Delineation and Disassociation. I had paid real-life, hard-to-come-by teenage money for this demo; my love was that deep. I was at that party for the sole purpose of staring at Daz, who a week earlier had told me he was in love with someone else, and so all I could feasibly do was watch him with a longing that made me breathless.

But then a skinny Black girl with a red scarf tied in her hair came up to me and said, breathlessly, "You are beautiful. You have to be a model!" I had never had a peer, definitely never a female, tell me I was beautiful. It felt so pure compared to the men who catcalled me or stared at my leggy teenage body. It was almost akin to reverence or prayer. I was floored. She brushed off my insistence that she was also gorgeous and repeated, "You"—she pointed—"you are beautiful." I don't think I thought about Daz the rest of the night.

We didn't meet again until Reading Festival when I, lost and overwhelmed and feeling out of place in this very white world of early-aughts rock festivals, bumped into Larissa. The relief washed over me. To this day whenever I am at some alt show amid a sea of white and see a Black or brown person I give a nod, a smile, maybe just share a look that means, yes, now there are two of us. When you are a teenager, what you want most, more than anything, is to belong. And I was no exception. I could never figure out how best to fit in, it always felt stilted and wrong, like jamming a puzzle piece in a place you know it doesn't go. I was awkward, I liked the wrong music and couldn't afford the right clothes, I was gawky and lanky and felt so conspicuous in my skin. Meeting Larissa that day gave me a little link in the chain, permission to be here, permission to join. That glimpse of her at the entrance of the festival was a glimpse of the many ways she would make me feel like I belonged in this galaxy.

Being a Black person and a fan in the overwhelmingly white rock scene is odd. You feel uninitiated and as if your dedication to the genre is not enough to surpass your Blackness. Much of this may just be my own personal shit, as I've been feeling this way since my Year 10 history teacher gave me all his Stiff Little Fingers CDs (not a euphemism but for sure a red flag); I know that the existence of almost every musical genre is rooted in Black history, I know that there are always Black people on the scene, I know that I am not alone in my love of a buzzing amp. But it often feels lonely. And every couple of years or so, a documentary comes out on some long-forgotten band like Bad Brains or Living Colour and everyone marvels at these pioneers and then relegates them back into the ash heap. It doesn't feel like there is a constant and steady Black rock scene and I need it, have needed it. There is often a person at the show who is loudly showing their knowledge of lyrics and I know the feeling because for me to be Black and quiet at these things was to feel like an imposter.

That's what was amazing about Larissa, she was able to be at home anywhere. Literally anywhere. Fancy restaurants in West London or Manhattan or Paris in vintage furs and Manolos of dubious origin, but also the dirtiest, stickiest bar full of skinheads. She oozed authenticity. She was so skinny in her skinny jeans, two long legs in ripped dark denim, a bandana around her wrist, a worn Sex Pistols shirt she had had since fifteen, cut up into fetching pieces. Black harness boots like moon boots securing her to this planet's surface because surely a girl who looked like this could defy gravity. She was alien and awe-inspiring but also somehow fit in with an ease I attempt to emulate to this day.

In our scene there were other nonwhite people, but we were most definitely the minority. Being Black in the clubs and bars we frequented was similar to being a celebrity in that everyone knew you, because you were hypervisible. Sometimes I think about Larissa's hair. In the scene we were in, the few Black girls (myself included) were straightening their hair, or wearing weave with severe asymmetric fringes to look like members of the Klaxons or the Strokes or Santigold or the Horrors or Crystal Castles. There was something defiant about Larissa's Afro pulled back into a timeless beehive, a trademark. She didn't give a shit, didn't try to fit in, didn't want to be whatever you thought cool was. She didn't care and it made everyone around her care more about her.

The men she dated fell into two camps—the first, sometimes rich, middle-aged men whom she didn't so much as kiss; the second (my favourite), punk boys, mod boys, skinny femme-looking boys. One such man, a beautiful ex-model with a shag cut and a history of famous women that would make the *Vanity Fair* society pages quake, was a flamenco guitarist. She once told me of the most rock and roll night she had ever had with him, rubbing shoulders with Mick Jones and Kate Moss and Jade Jagger, those bastions of British rock and roll, a long night of debauchery and too-loud music and the promise of sex. Larissa would always find herself in these situations—suddenly in the loos becoming best friends with Debbie Harry. She wasn't a beg friend, Larissa, no. Somehow these famous people thought she must be famous too, she exuded such a legitimacy, such an air of belonging, there was no pretense, this was just who she was and so the celebrities assumed she did indeed belong.

She was briefly friends with Amy Winehouse, despite never even having listened to her music. Larissa would go to Amy's house for these big, lavish lunches she would put on. She didn't talk about it to me in detail until after Amy died and we watched aerial footage of her body being taken out of her house. She was twenty-seven. We were obsessed with that number. It seemed so young. I didn't know then that thirty-two would feel pretty young, too.

She wasn't a gossip. Not about things she cared about. I could trust her with so much, she knew so many secrets. She was friends with a lot of celebrities whose names I shall spare you, as Larissa would have wanted it that way. She knew their dirty habits, knew their dark secrets and she carried them to the grave.

Sometimes when I am nervous, at a show or a party where I know no one and feel like a fraud, I try to channel Larissa. I think about what she would be saying to me were she there, something like "Come on, shmooms, you look like a smoke-show, someone is bound to buy you a drink. Everyone here wants to talk to you, they're just too intimidated! Stand up straight and stop looking concerned," and sometimes it works. Sometimes I will take off my jacket, revealing the dress that felt amazing in my bedroom but feels too much now, I will order the martini, I will look bored and pretend she is right there with me, bolstering me, making me seem as legit as she was.

Larissa <larry67@xmail.com>   Mar 4, 2013,
to me   10:00 AM

Oh my god you are the cutest thing in the
wholee wide world!!!!! I wanna hug you so
much after seeing those pics! Oh my god
your smile is sooooooooooooo cute! Poopoo
why are you the most beautiful girl in the
world?!!!!!

Larissa <larry67@xmail.com>   Mar 4, 2013,
to me   10:01 AM

Oh my god yore so cute! So so so so
pretty!!!!

Eirinie <eirinieeee@xmail.com>   Mar 4, 2013,
to Larissa   10:21 AM

Pfffffffffffffffft!
You're ridic. I look like a beige moonface!
I thought you should see them though!
How's work btw??? Do you have an agency
now???

—

Sent from my iPad

TV PRESENTER

We had a friend (or rather, she was your friend who barely tolerated me) who was a famous TV presenter in the UK. She was cool, knew cool people, did cool shit, lived in a cool flat near Old Street. She was always surrounded by men, all her friends were men, a red flag if ever there was one. She seemed threatened by certain women and, although at the time I was just a shy, insecure girl, I was one of the women whose presence unsettled her. You would still take me with you to certain parties where she would talk to you at length, barely giving me a glance. If any man she knew ever talked to me she would expertly intercept and do something crazily brazen like turn her back on me, shit I would not tolerate today but back then, at nineteen, twenty, I figured this was my worth anyway, it was merely verification. What did I have to say that would merit attention?

She thought, as many people did with you, that you were best friends. You had a way of making people confide in you, making them think you were their person. You were so fucking cool it was as if they couldn't believe their luck that they had your attention, and so if they had indeed caught it then it must mean something, when really I knew that it merely meant you were temporarily entertained by them. You loved a big personality, particularly in women. Loud, bright, fun, reckless women. I was always confused with what you saw in me, particularly at that time when I thought about every move I made three times over before I actually took action, doubted myself at every turn. The TV presenter was one of the other types of women, brash and rich and the centre of the party, and for about a year most of our extracurricular activities happened with or around her.

She trusted you so much that sometimes she would even give you her Coutts card, that exclusive bank in London that only takes accounts containing a minimum of £500,000, or £5 million in assets. She'd send you to the ATM, you'd take wads of cash out, later you'd tell Maddy just how insane it was that this presenter trusted you. Not that you ever stole from her, to my knowledge, but I know that it crossed your mind just in a power way. Just in a "the things I could do" way. And with me you would always bring me in, include me. You saw the way the presenter excluded and seemed extra puffed up around me, it was clear to you long before it was clear to me, although in hindsight, looking at photos of nineteen-year-old me yeah holy shit I was a babe, I'd have been threatened too. But you were always an arm around my shoulder to bring me in, you made her include me even when it was very clear she would rather not.

You were such a doorway to so many aspects of my adulthood, you facilitated so many moments that caused me to reassess who I was, who I wanted to be. I think back on this time with the TV presenter, about how unpleasant she was to me, about how kind she was to you, and I realise this helped me decide what treatment I would accept from people. These events were brought, like offerings, to me, by you. Because of you I flourished. Because of you another part of me solidified in that way it does when you are young and coming into yourself. Because of you I am me.

Last night

....

Eirinie <eirinieeee@xmail.com >   Nov 23, 2013,
to Larissa   12:14 PM

Adam and I went to see porgy and Bess!
the Gershwin opera and I missed you so
dreadfully.

I'm going to tell you all the things I
miss about you:
I miss how sometimes you'd come home and
have a dress or something that you thought
would look good on me and make me try it
on for you
I miss how you'd suggest books for me
because I have the hardest time doing it
for myself
I miss languorous hangovers where we would
order take out and watch movies all day
and have naps and never feel bad about it
I miss how you'd take fucking FOREVER to
get ready to go out, even if I gave you
two hours warning
I miss how we could get anything we wanted
from men and give nothing in return
I miss being partners in crime at dinners
at the Ivy and all those fancy restaurants
we we're take to
I miss having late night calls from you
when I was at work asking when I'd be home
I miss you making me food
I miss you calling me shmoomalates and
telling me I'm pretty
I miss feeling the most comfortable I
have ever felt around another woman, and
the very little effort we had to put into
knowing each other so well

:)

End

—
Sent from my iPad

....

Larissa <larry67@xmail.com>   Dec 1, 2013,
to me   7:59 AM

So rude that I'm only replying now to your
very lovely email thankyou
How's everything? I'm in Berlin at mo – I
swear feels like I been here for years! I
miss Paris and French people and French
everything!! It's really hard to feel
normal in a city you don't know… How's
states?? Are you properly settled now) I
mean obvs you were before but you know
what I mean. Is it different being married
do you think? Or feels same at home and
stuff?
What have you been up to?
I've been sleeping loads and waking up at
3!!! Hahaha
When will I see you again???
I miss all those things you said too!!!
That's funny :)
Xxxxxxxxx

I DON'T LIKE YOU

There were things I didn't like about you. You weren't perfect. You could be stubborn in a truly baffling way, immovable as solid marble, there was nothing you could be made to do, except maybe by your mother.

You were bad with money, but then that's a bit pot calling the kettle black, isn't it? I was also bad with money, I suppose all people in their early twenties are, but sometimes you would prioritise a fancy meal over our looming rent. Sometimes we would both forget the essentials, the adult responsibilities we were supposed to be paying attention to, and as a result our finances were chaotic, our rent was always late, our tab always paid for in shrapnel.

Your silences could be isolating. I understood them, sure, but that didn't mean I wasn't often devastated by their coldness. Didn't mean I wasn't often swallowing down my own feelings because I knew they would be met with a stony quiet.

You were selfish. It was primarily about you, everything was about what you wanted, and so I had to shift myself over to accommodate, to make sure you were attended to. Sometimes I felt like a lady in waiting, and sure you were a glamourous queen to wait upon, but I was second tier, I was supporting role, I was your partner in crime when I wanted to be you, wanted to be the fulcrum.

You could be reclusive. Not that this is inherently bad, I suppose, but at times, when mixed with your stubbornness, it meant we could go days without seeing each other even when we lived in the same flat, even when you were only a hallway away. You were content by yourself and it often forced me to find a way to be like that too, although I never found true solace in solitude until my late twenties. But you could lock yourself away, resisting replying to me through the door. I was often shut out of your world, out of your head.

Even when living, time meant almost nothing to you. You were always, always late. A meetup time? A suggestion. A deadline? A lap line to be crossed at your leisure. I was forever apologising for us not being on time, I was forever sitting in the living room waiting for you to get ready, I would be fully dressed and made up whilst you dusted the naptime sleep from your eyes and meandered lazily to the shower. It wasn't quite disrespect, I knew that, but at times it felt as if what I wanted, the schedule I kept, was completely invisible to you.

I think it is important to remember the shitty things about you, Larissa. I don't want you to be a saint. I don't want to lie about the type of person you were, so many of the pure joys of knowing you lie side by side with some of your worst faults. I want to be honest about this. I want, if you are listening from wherever dead people

listen from, you to feel some contrition about how you often be-
haved, even to me, even to a longtime best friend.

Your attention could swivel quickly. You always had a shiny
new person who was introducing you around, taking you to new
places. You liked the new and the shiny. Which often meant you
would pivot away from me, temporarily distracted for a week or
a month or however long it took before the new-new pissed you
off, because they always did. People didn't always take the time to
observe you, not properly. They didn't see the invisible land mines,
the boundaries never to be crossed, the soft and fragile parts of you
to be handled with care, and so they inevitably fucked up and you
inevitably came back to me, and your other true blues. I suppose I
did this too. It wasn't like I was hanging on your every word. But I
didn't pivot so readily from you. Not until the end. And even then,
I didn't know why I was so keen to look away.

Now I know I didn't want to bear witness to what, I am sure,
somewhere inside me, I knew was a steady demise. Was it revenge,
this sudden turning of my head? To get you back for all the times
my emails went unanswered, for the times you were too busy to
talk or to meet? When I look over those final messages it sure
seems like that. A willful ignorance, a shutting tight of my eyes.

Was that me, regaining control at the end? Finally telling you
I wouldn't be bossed about by your moods, wouldn't be the baby
anymore, wouldn't be subservient. In the light of everything that
happened, of how you died, I now see you needed my knowledge
of you, needed me to pay closer attention so that I could help. So
that you could let yourself be helped. It seems foolish, blind even,

that I didn't lift a finger at the end. But then again, you had done your signature move, you had shut the door in my face and I hadn't bothered to wonder what was behind it, what was the reason you didn't want me looking. If I had, maybe I could have stopped you. Maybe I could have intervened.

I fluctuate between thinking I could have helped you in any way and seeing the reality of the situation, the reality of who you were. All of the flaws mentioned above were precisely why I couldn't help you. Your selfishness, your tardiness, your reclusiveness—these were the things that were barriers. Things you purposefully constructed to keep people out, and they worked well, too well. In the end maybe I was a bit fatigued by your peculiarities, I didn't have time to cater to your whims. Maybe in the end we were both flawed.

I like to believe that you would have asked me outright for help, if you'd had the courage. I like to believe you would have known that the understanding and space I always gave you would have been valid currency, even when faced with the truth of you, the truth of your life then. But maybe not. Maybe you had so barricaded yourself into your own mind that you forgot, temporarily (a glaring error), that I had the capacity to understand you. Maybe you had been reclusive for so long you truly believed you were on your own. You weren't, because I haven't even left your side now, and you've been dead for over two years. You weren't, because I would never leave you.

Larissa <larry67@xmail.com>   May 18, 2009,
to me   9:46 AM

Hi where are you? I actually hate everyone
else. Come back to me x x x x

I FEEL LIKE

A MESS SOME DAYS

I feel like a mess some days. Most days. I feel as if I should be doing better. No one talks about her, no one asks how I am doing. The flush of flowers and condolence texts made me think that perhaps grieving was permitted, that my mood was warranted. Suddenly those dried up and now I assume that I should be over it, that I should be laced up and fine in public. No one asks about her.

Should I be fine? I don't feel fine. Should I be over it? I don't feel over it. I want to be, I want to not feel the sting of tears in my eyes, I want to not excuse myself to go to the bathroom and do some deep breathing exercises to keep from spiraling. I want to have something in common with these people at work, these friends I meet for drinks, I want to be able to be genuine and feel love and joy and smile and forget but I can't. I leave sobbing voicemails on Larry's phone in the cab home, I am filled with dread every time I call that this might be the time I hear "the number you have dialed has not been recognised" and every time I get through to the voicemail, I begin my recording with a sigh of relief. It's not logical, this voice-mail obsession. No one can hear them, more specifically she cannot hear them. Whatever channel I think I am opening, whatever portal to the beyond, is all in my head. There is no one in this cab with me but the driver who is politely pretending not to hear.

What am I supposed to do with my grief? At least with these voice-mails they feel filed away, it seems as if I have put them in the final spot the universe has reserved for these feelings.

Sometimes I whisper them into my phone in the dark, at night, in bed. Or I text, voice note. Penance to an empty confessional booth. I do not pause to examine whether this is a healthy thing to do, I trudge on and make my tiny deposit of sadness in the hopes it will allow me to move on, but it doesn't help as much as I'd like it to. Somewhere in my brain, in the illogical, magical portion of it, I hope to be surprised by the picking up of the phone, suddenly your voice from somewhere, I would stutter and stumble for sure but the connection would have been made. The life preserver, thrown out over and over and over again, would have been grabbed from the other side and you or maybe I would be able to pull the other in, but which side I'd prefer I am not sure.

My brain feels chaotic. It is a jumbled mess that I must use to get through the minutiae of the day—feed my child, go to work, bathe, eat, socialise. Somehow, I manage to get these things done, despite the certainty in my skull that I won't be able to get up, won't be able to eat, won't be able to laugh. Somehow, I do. Mostly I achieve this by pushing my feelings down, deep, deep down to a place where the pain is still felt but is muffled by everything else I put on top of it, like a pile of coats in the spare room at a party that soon become indistinguishable from the bed itself.

I do not mention this method I have to my therapist; I know what she will say. She will tell me it's not healthy to squash every-thing down, that I have to allow myself to feel the sadness but really, I would retort if I ever got up the courage to tell Julie this, how the fuck is anyone supposed to do that? It is not feasible in this cold world we have created to make the space for oneself, to allow one-self to cry in public, to make colleagues uncomfortable with one's rawness, to scare one's child with an unprovoked rage at the world. If I want to be any sort of functioning human, if I intend to keep my life as I like it (correction, liked it, before Larissa died), how the fuck am I supposed to behave? I didn't make these rules, I didn't say that it was inappropriate to cry to the waiter at lunch because they suggested a house cocktail that Larissa would have loved, I didn't say that clutching all of her clothes to my chest and getting into bed was an unhealthy way to be. I am just here, living in the world you people created, following the rules so I don't embarrass anyone.

But the truth is I want to scream, I want to do all of those things, I want my sadness to be noticed like it was in those days of flower deliveries and "I'm so sorry" texts. I want to be babied, I want deliveries of soups and casseroles, I want to feel safe in my sorrow, I want to be able to scream and have everyone nod and agree that this is okay and fine and necessary. But instead, here I am, pushing it all down. What else would you have me do, Julie? I have to eat, I have to make a living, I have to keep fucking going don't we all have to keep fucking going?

The indulgence therapy tells us to take just isn't feasible all the time. I can't be sad all the time, can I? Who is it helping, who am I helping with all this anger, all this bemusement, all this lost lost lost— ness, all this fucking sobbing down defunct phone lines? I am not sure I am even helping myself. I am not sure I know how to do that.

I start taking walks with my dog, only ever by myself, only ever the two of us. I prefer the beach but a trail will do too, somewhere slightly secluded. I like it because I can talk to myself, or rather, to you. I talk about nothing in particular, I usually don't even cry, they are banal conversations, the sorts of things we would be talk- ing about if you were still alive. At first on these walks I start by not moving my lips too much just in case a passerby should see me and think, "Poor thing, she's insane." But after a few outings I feel bolstered by the presence of my dog, as if he is an explanation for my ramblings on the Soho club scene in 2006, or my recollec- tions of our adventures together, long nights and pricey cocktails, cozy movie days and Marilyn Monroe on the screen. I start talking more boldly. I begin to tell you about my life, I tell you how proud you would be of my daughter, how funny she is, how stubborn. I know you would particularly like the stubborn part, you loved a woman who knew her mind, knew where to draw the line. I know you would love her.

I wax lyrical about her, about us, about Adam, about life. I scold you for not being here, as if you are just late for dinner (as you often were) instead of being dead, buried in the ground in Paris so far from me. It feels nice. It feels crazy. It feels sort of nice to feel sort of crazy.

There is something so cathartic in giving in to the madness. I am starting to understand what Julie wanted from me, she wanted some space, not all of it, not my whole day but just some space for me to be crazy. For me to feel unhinged. For me to do things that would make me feel like I was plunging off the deep end a little, madness-wise. I need to feel that crazed because that is the only time I am honest with my feelings, the only time I truly indulge in my insanity. And so, I do not take my whole day and upend it, but rather, I carve out an hour, sometimes two or three, to be batshit. And no one can judge me, not even the dog.

Communing with you in this way feels ten times as good as the voicemails and voice notes, I am not whispering into the line or feeling guilt at my madness, instead I am strolling wide strides and talking with an assurance, as if I know you can hear, as if I am certain. And with that I am also striding into my grief, so much of which right now feels like pure insanity. I have to go in, I have to get crazy or else how will I ever speak to you ever again? Surely the universe can allow me this. Surely this is better than the alternative.

One day almost two years later Larissa's mum will confess to me that she remembered she had Larry's phone and turned it on to read the messages, find some clues. It will only occur to me later that perhaps in doing so she also found my voicemails, and so that perhaps the reason it felt at the time like a portal to the beyond was because it was, but not to the person I thought it would be. It was a portal to the future, and in the future your bereft mother might play my voicemails, hear my broken heart, hear my deep love and loss of you, and perhaps, in some small way, be comforted.

....

Eirinie <eirinieeee@xmail.com>   Jun 2, 2015
to Larissa

POOOOOOO

On Monday, June 1, 2015, Larissa
<Larry67@xmail.com> wrote:
        Hi

....

Eirinie <eirinieeee@xmail.com>   Jun 2, 2015
to Larissa

What you doing what you saying?!

....

Larissa <larry67@xmail.com>   Jun 5, 2015
to me

Hi poo poo love you xxxxxxcx

....

Eirinie <eirinieeee@xmail.com>   Jun 5, 2015
to Larissa

HI POO POO HEAD!
I love YOU

....

I THINK I AM READY

I ask my therapist for advice on starting a grief group. I think I am ready. It has only been four months but I assume I am ready. Julie tells me that it is a burden, starting a group like that. She worries that I'm doing something so expansive and collective I will find myself with little time to grieve, something I am already struggling with.

"Where is the time for you?" she asks. Where, she wonders, does my sadness and processing fit in between my obligations as a mother, my job that requires a cheerful demeanor, my life, and now these strangers I am suggesting to add? I don't have an answer for her. I didn't think of it like that, I only thought, if I could be around other sad people, other bereft people, I might feel less crazy all the time. Maybe someone else in the group would also know my preoccupation with death, imagining it constantly, seeing all the ways I or people I love could die, as if thinking of them would make me prepared. Maybe if I heard

someone else talk this way I would think, oh, I'm okay, this is
normal at least here in this room.

I am not good at centring myself in conversations. I ask the
questions; I wonder about your job and pull your family tree out
of you and convince you to tell me things you don't usually tell
strangers. I am good at making space for others but in doing so I
rarely leave space for me. I often find myself up against the wall,
breathing in so as to minimise the size of me, muttering, "You,
you, you" but rarely "I."

So, Julie is right. When you are in your grief it is hard to also
make space for someone else's, inevitably the conversation will
turn to your dead, your beloved, your forever gone. How would
I keep that balance? I am not a trained therapist I am not impartial
to the subject I am not objective I am very much in it. I realise that
starting the group as a lifeline for myself might not be a good idea,
what with everyone else casting a lifeline into the group at the
same time. Who would do the rescuing?

Everything is so murky after Larissa died, no one knows anything and she was so young and not a planner, nothing is known
about what she would have wanted. It scares me. It makes me blurt
out to my husband, whenever I particularly feel my mortality, my
last rites. I want to be cremated. I want Billy Idol played at my funeral. I don't want God talked about profusely, it would ring false
just as it did at Larissa's funeral, it is not something that was part of
my life and so it would be jarring to hear it. I tell my husband that
although we frequently joke about him never marrying again after
me, like Joe DiMaggio, I do want him to find someone. I want

him to have support, I don't want him to be sad forever, I want our child to have another parent, I want life to be as good as it could be for them. But what did Larissa want? What does she want from us, those left behind? She never told me. I don't know what she wants, what she would want me to do. I can assume but I wish she had left me some clue to my purpose without her. I wish I knew what to do.

It is frustrating when the one person who could answer all of your many, many questions is the dead person. Would she laugh kindly at the idea of my grieving, say "Oh Eirins, it's all okay, I'm dead, I don't care what you do or how you remember me"? Or would she say "Memorialise me, worship me, don't fucking forget"?

Larissa <larry67@xmail.com>   Feb 21, 2012
to me

wher r u
like actually

Eirinie <eirinieeee@xmail.com>   Feb 21, 2012
to Larissa

Just got home, about to go to work.
Whats up shmoo???

Xxx

Larissa <larry67@xmail.com>   Feb 21, 2012
to me

urgh
EVERYTHING!!!!
i hate men
REALLY do!!! just wanna let off some steam
is all :(
and just need to speak to you
NOW!!!!

EAST FINCHLEY

It's raining here. A spring shower, the kind that starts and finishes in less than twenty minutes. I like this kind of rain, it reminds me of being somewhere tropical, like Jamaica or Hawaii—that frantic outburst of rain like a shout or a cry in the middle of the blue sky. There is something cathartic about it to me, something freeing. How I'd like to feel, sometimes, that outburst, that unsanctioned scream. And then, suddenly, over, and the sky is blue again and it is as if it never happened, the only clue is the green of the plants that are now alive with wetness.

It makes me think of the flat in East Finchley, with that surprising garden, a backyard of British greens. It was way too good for us, we got it through sheer luck and pandering, it was on a nice quiet residential street at the weird end of the northbound Northern line, one tube and hardly any buses. The house was a duplex, below lived a middle-aged couple and their autistic son, and upstairs was a two-ish-bedroom flat, spacious. Bamboo furniture in the front room made it feel like you had fled the city to Spain or somewhere, there were floor-to-ceiling sliding doors that looked out onto a terrace and beyond that, a series of lush green gardens. It was a transformative space. The first time we saw it, after weeks of looking at pokey flats with zero natural light, zero outdoor space, we were immediately in love. True to our style it was out of our monthly budget by a good couple of hundred pounds, true to our style once we set our hearts on it, we couldn't backpedal.

A nice Jewish man who was leaving London for Tel Aviv agreed to rent to us, we fluffed up our finances, made them look more impressive than the reality of being a scarcely employed model and a subordinate in a small publishing house actually would. I took the bigger room, the one with the Jacuzzi tub and private bathroom. We asked my friend Charlie if she wanted a small room, tiny really, for discounted rent, and she accepted.

Everyone who visited said it was like being on holiday, coming to our flat. The terra-cotta floors of the front room, the greenness filtering through the glass, it didn't feel like London at all. That's probably why we liked it. We had so many parties there, tolerated by our downstairs neighbours, who said they were just happy to have people who wouldn't complain about the loud and unexpected sounds their son would make in frustration or happiness or sadness. It didn't bother us; we didn't sleep normal hours and so an outburst in the night wasn't as disruptive as it might have been to people who worked more conventional hours five days a week. We never really saw the teen, save for sunny days when he bounced on a trampoline in their yard, giddy happy sounds then, a boy of maybe seventeen.

We rarely thought about how lucky we were back then, but that house was a find. Of course, the bamboo furniture was wildly uncomfortable, just glorified patio furniture, and the light that streamed in during those long summer days was unflinching, we had no blinds. The plumbing in the house was old, toilets and showers backed up, the terra-cotta floors were cold in the morning, slippers or bed socks were the only way to survive in the winter. And we had never had such a big place, we underestimated the amount it cost to heat it, to keep it running. We were the youngest people on the street by miles, for sure, and stood out.

It is one of those times that, as an established and settled adult, I look back on with a fondness, a rosy haze. I forget the poverty, the crippling monthly financial stress of rent and bills, the desire to have fun adventures that were almost always cost-prohibitive. And now that Larissa is dead it feels even more magical, it feels like a time we were in a bubble together, formative months for our friendship. That was the time I felt the closest to you, that was the time I was the most me and you were the most you. It is nostalgic the way the smell of the rain is nostalgic; it was cold and miserable and thoroughly British at the time, but now all I remember is the wet earth, the cleansing and quenching, the buds opening on trees, becoming possibilities.

Larissa <larry67@xmail.com>   Apr 25, 2011,
to me   3:44 AM

Am Just DEVORURING mitford letters. Really
they are great. You must read, so funny
and entertaining and full of heart. Am
almost fin but don't want to get to the
end because she died in 1973 and I'm on
the letters of 1971!! O no! Nancy don't
go!!!!! Xxx

CHAPTER 15

DEATH ON MY MIND

I think a lot about you, but not in a close-up way. I think about how you died, but not in an investigative sort of way. I frequently think about what Pierre and Simon must have seen when they found you. I've never seen a dead body before, not really, not one that wasn't dolled up in a coffin with nowhere to go. I can only imagine, and I do, what a body would look like after a week in a bathtub.

"She didn't look like herself," Simon had said on a muffled call from Paris a few days after you were found. He sounded like he was walking fast, breathless. He sounded out of his mind, he sounded scared, he sounded sick.

I think about that a lot.

I do not think about the hows or whys. I do not ask what pills you took, what people thought might have happened. I don't want to

know and I want to know. Sometimes it seems like I truly want to
know and I try to look head-on at what happened to you and when
I do that sometimes, sometimes it feels like there is something for
me to see flitting just out of vision, skirting the peripheries, but I
can't seem to get my head to move fast enough to catch it.

There are rarely times I am not thinking about you, I am con-
sumed. And if it is not you directly, then it is the death, the loss of
life, the insanity of the suddenness of it all that I fixate on. When
driving on the freeway I imagine what would happen if I were to
get in an accident, if the car were to flip and I were catapulted out
onto hard, hot LA asphalt. The possibility of this seems closer than
it did before, before you were dead. The proximity of mortality is
inching ever closer in this new, post-Larissa world. Walking home
at night from my therapist's office, I think about being stabbed. I
think about it in great detail, how it might feel to have a blade in-
serted with force into my body, how much blood there would be,
if I would be able to call for help. I think about dying in my sleep.
Who would find me? Would it be my child? My husband? Would
they ever get over that?

It sounds as if I am fantasising about dying, as if I have what a
doctor would call suicidal ideations, but I am not. I feel as though it
is my job to think of these things, to make sure I catalog every possible way I could leave my family alone and devastated. It is not a
fantasy; I do not want this. I just don't want to be caught out again.

Why hadn't I been prepared for your death, before? Why hadn't
I thought about what it might be like to lose someone so dear to me?

Why hadn't I been prepared? Although in all honesty I am not sure what that preparedness would have looked like. I spent a long time knowing my grandmother would eventually die of the breast and then bone cancer that riddled her, and yet I don't ever remember feeling ready for her to go. I think I was in denial, I think I was too young to really understand the finality of the moment, and so, when she finally died, I was taken aback. I thought there was more time.

And my dad, not a wonderful father figure, not a present man in my life, not stable or reliable in any way one would desire from a parent. The one truth I knew about him was that one day, some day in the future, I would get a call telling me he was dead. And that would be the extent of my communication with him: sporadic, belated birthday messages, a few well-intentioned texts, and a death notice from a distant relative. I knew this was likely and yet, the day that he had his aneurysms and was carted off to intensive care, when my mother called and told me to get on a plane to say goodbye, I was caught unawares again. I knew this, I knew this was coming and so why was I surprised? Why did my head begin to make a hurried list of all the things I needed to say to him, all the things we had yet to air out?

In the end, my father didn't die that day. He survived, much to the doctor's surprise, and with more mobility and motor functions than would have been expected in a man his age after such a series of brain bleeds. He didn't die but he lost a great deal of his memory, he lost the ability to connect the mental dots needed to atone for his actions, and I lost the ability to hold him accountable. Not dead then, but not what I needed.

Our neighbour across the street is sick. She is older, she has cancer and has been fighting it for about a year. My family and some of the other families on our block have been making her sporadic meals, staying cheery, stopping too long to chat with her and her husband as they get in their daily walk at a sloth's pace. Now that it is the end of her life, they kindly asked for no more food, no more drop-ins. She is dying. Our quiet street is crowded with cars, her friends and family have gathered day and night, she and her husband are not alone.

I am sure her family would disagree, but this seems like a nice way to die. Not the cancer, not the prolonged and exhaustive chemo, not the hair loss and the loss of appetite, but this coming together of everyone you love, this community even in the depths of sadness. That must be nice. I wish I could have given you that, Larissa. I would have liked to have found your favourite foods, I would have liked to have brought you flowers you could see and smell instead of whatever wilted ones I will leave on your grave whenever I next get to Paris. I would have liked to have been forewarned, I guess. I would have liked to have been the constant at your bedside as you were dying, weathering all the fake friends and looky-loos and people we once would have laughed at after they'd left the room. I'd have liked that. I'm sure you would have too.

It haunts me, the idea of you alone. The idea that I didn't know. The idea that no one knew. I would have liked to have eased the pain. I would have liked to have held your hand.

I don't know, can you ever be ready? Can you ever brace for

impact? I have a friend who watched her father die in her home, a slow death caused by some kind of brain tumor that slowly robbed him of any semblance of who he was. She and her family were his nurses and it was tough, laborious work that left her completely depleted at the end of the day. She worked like this for about a year before her father finally died. She lived every day with the knowledge that the man she loved was not going to recover, that the end was growing closer, and even with this foresight she was devastated in a way that she said surprised her. And so no, probably not. You probably can't prepare. You can't get the emotions out beforehand, wring them out like a washcloth so that you are dry and useful to everyone after the funeral, so you can clear glasses and pat hands and make sure everyone got their chance to say their piece (peace?) instead of sobbing into a wineglass, begging for a drunkenness that refuses to come.

Have you ever tried to get drunk but had some kind of mental block? It's maddening. Your brain won't let you; it knows this isn't what you need and yet you guzzle anyway and it's fucking pointless because even a bottle of wine doesn't get you the sort of drunk you need to be to believe that everything is fine and happy again.

At my grandmother's funeral I drank so much. So much. No one said anything, I think because they were too busy drinking themselves. I was young though, twenty, I think, maybe nineteen. Probably should have had someone intervene but no one did and so I stole a bottle of port. Sherry? Something bizarre to my young palate that had been brought as a gift and I took it outside and I think I drank it on my own. I felt nothing but the overwhelming desire to fill myself up with something, some feeling some semblance of something that wasn't just excruciating pain and the holding back of tears. I wore an old dress of my mother's, people said I looked lovely, I thought that was an inappropriate thing to say. I didn't want to look lovely, I wanted to look how I felt inside, which was broken and adrift and desperate.

At Larissa's funeral I tried to drink, tried to numb, tried to get in the celebratory mindset that some of the guests at the wake seemed to be in. Larissa would have wanted a party, that's for sure. She would have wanted a bright glowy well-dressed party, she would have wanted me drunk, I thought. And so, I did my best. But again, the feeling of abandon I was searching for didn't come, again I was just lost, in a room full of people, feeling completely empty.

I think of my funeral sometimes. What I would want ("Dancing with Myself" playing), whom I would want there (everyone who would be genuinely, appropriately sad), what I would want worn (black, of course). I think about this a lot because I feel it is my duty to think about it. Because despite everything I have just said, despite everything I have learnt to the contrary, if I think about it enough then when the end comes for me, I will have been ready. I will have been at peace. I will be accepting.

I wonder if Larissa was accepting. Did she know, at the end? She was sad a lot, she had broken up with a very beautiful man who had cheated on her rampantly, told her to her face in the most French way possible that he didn't feel anything for her. She was sad, she was writing songs and poetry that were depressed and pessimistic. Was this her way of clearing the way for her own death?

Did she feel the end was close? Or was she just a young broken-hearted woman who was trying to cure herself, who needed help but wouldn't ask for it? Was she as surprised as the rest of us when she died? I don't know.

I do know, however, that for me, right now, it is comforting to think of death. It is comforting to imagine my body mangled beyond recognition in a horrific accident, to imagine falling down the stairs even, hitting my head and dying later at a hospital. I feel sort of in control when I think about these things, I feel like I have the knowledge, the knowledge to protect myself and my family, to brace for impact, to steel ourselves for this eventuality we all live with but somehow forget every single day. It was only with Larissa's death that I began to realise how close the end is, how if you just reach out a curious hand you may touch it, cold and final, and know that it is for you, too.

Larissa <larry67@xmail.com>   Jul 21, 2013,
to me   3:00 AM

Oh no
Have u made doc appointment? Only thing
to get better is antibiotic. Better now
then in couple weeks! Are u back in London
then? With flat mates from hell?? When
are you leaving there? Moving to San Fran
finally!
Hope you feel better soon
Xxx

Eirinie <eirinieeee@xmail.com>   Jul 21, 2013,
to Larissa   3:04 PM

Shmoomies?

I think my beautiful man is coming to see
you if you're still at the bar!
Omg I can't believe you were gonna invite
him to a pool party; cheers dude, get my
fiancé around lots of beautiful French
bikini girls! :)

I am so so jealous that he's there, I want
to be there with you!
I cannot wait to see your beautiful face
in August. I'm going to SQUEEZE YOU!

—

Sent from my iPad

MEMORY

Two years. Two years of me thinking about you being dead, referring to you in the past tense. Sometimes you are so firmly "back there" that I have to tell your stories just to remind myself what you were like. It's slipping a bit, the active and vivid memories of you, and that frightens me so much because my god you were amazing. I don't want to forget how amazing you were. I don't want to get numb to that part of you. I feel as if by not immersing myself fully in our past, your past, I am fucking up. I am forgetting.

I can't afford to forget.

How to remember? Is it enough just to write this book? To faithfully, accurately sketch out the key moments in our lives together, the key aspects of your personality, the things that made you the most unique person I have ever known? Is this enough? At what point does it become a dispassionate collection of recollections, at what point is it just ink on paper? Am I doing enough? Am I capturing those minuscule particles? Is it even possible to gather those fairy-dust remnants and commit them to paper so that someone else, someone who didn't know the magic of you, will be able to feel your electricity?

Or is this futile? Is the exercise of remembering doing more harm than good?

I heard a podcast once where they discussed how memory, at its most preserved and pristine, had to be untouched and unremembered to be as true as it can be. A real Catch-22, the very act of remembering taints the memory, we add little details here and there, embellish without being aware, emotions come into play, hindsight helps to clarify the blurry and before we know it, we have desecrated a pure memory. In the act of remembering we are unremembering.

Is that what I am doing with you? Am I trying to scribble this all down before my own human tendencies taint it all? Or is it too late for that, have I already trodden all over the crime scene, tampered with the evidence? In that case, this book becomes less about you and more about me every day.

Who would I be had you not died? Who would we be? I've compiled all these emails and stories but the truth is we had been distant, physically and emotionally, for a while. We were only just getting back to that ease, that casualness. I have a thousand voice notes I wish I could cram into these pages from the last two years of your life, but would we have ever regained that intimacy? We probably would never have lived together again, never would have come home to each other, full of a cosy relief.

Who would you have been past the age of thirty-two? I imagine there will be a time when I am at an age I'd have liked to see you at, fifty, for example. Who would you have been as a fifty-year-old woman?

That is the most everlasting pain of grief, I think, the never-ending wondering. No more new memories. It is so complete. What was, is the loss. What could have been, is the loss. Past, present, and future, I am bereft and I'm not sure how I reconcile that. Perhaps I merely warm my hands on the image of you as an old woman, crotchety yet stylish, the kind of auntie my children are afraid of when they are young but, as they get older, fear shifts to awe. A surprising elderly lady, prone to pulling Veuve out of her handbag, a smoker of cigarettes. Those eyes of yours watching the world turn and change, smiling as if you already knew it all.

I recently got some new photos back from an old shoot. I liked them, despite the fact my newly emerged pregnancy bump was dwarfing my body, despite the fact I have a hard time remembering that it is okay, good even, for my body to change during this time. I thought I looked pretty. Beautiful even. I had a strange, knee-jerk reaction to the photos where I began to forward them to you. I saved the photos, I clicked send message, and then I remembered. I wasn't even sad about it. It felt like what I imagine phantom limb pain feels like. A reach down for a scratch of the calf, a realisation it's not there. Nothing to itch, nothing to scratch. Remembering. You are my phantom limb now.

Do people who experience this type of physical loss often have PTSD? Do they ever freak out, screaming in the night that their arm or leg isn't there? Does that last forever, that screaming, or does it become a quick shake of the psyche, a reminder that everything is fine, there is just no forearm now? Days and years spent prior to whatever accident, not even acknowledging the privilege of having all your appendages. Swimming and high-fiving or kicking a football or playing footsie with someone, all whilst oblivious of the tenuous nature of our lives on Earth. I can only imagine what it is like through this experience with you.

You feel, now, as essential to me as a limb. Did I think that back then, though? Often, I punish myself, wonder if I did enough, if I felt enough. Sometimes even whilst writing this I wonder if I am embellishing, if it's true what I am writing. Did we love one another like I insist we did? Am I misremembering? How much damage am I doing simply by remembering if indeed remembering does the damage those scientists believe it to? If every time I remember you I am adding my own colours, my own voice to something that must remain neutral in order to maintain its integrity.

Am I wallowing?

And then I see something, perhaps a photo, or perhaps a voice note from you, and I hear the love in your voice, I hear you calling me "shmooms," I hear you laughing at my slutty jokes, I see an old video of us and I think, no, I am not wrong. That's how it was. We loved each other in that way that sisters do—a casualness with each other that is hard to fake, a closeness that made others uncomfortable, an affectionate, demonstrative love at times. An in-joke kind of love, a teasing love, a stone-cold truth kind of love. A "share the cute photos of yourself" kind of love.

There aren't enough videos of the two of us. I would love more. I want to see with my own eyes that bond we had. I want someone else to bear witness to it, not just me, not just fucking me. Because now that's all it is, it's me standing as a testament to our love. Just me, on my jays, dictating how it was. I want something more, I want an audience, I want a crowd to nod and say, yes, we see it, you didn't imagine it, it's real. It was your appendage, you took it for granted but you loved it, and you missed it when it was gone.

It's just not there anymore.

moomles

. . . .

 Eirinie <eirinieeee@xmail.com>   Apr 20, 2011
to Larissa

are those your potats in the fridge?
May i eat one?
x

. . . .

 Larissa <larry67@xmail.com>   Apr 20, 2011
to me

Yes mine. Yes eat.

ONLY if you make some for me too. Don't
worry I like cold food! Xx

. . . .

 Eirinie <eirinieeee@xmail.com>   Apr 20, 2011
to Larissa

i was gonna make a baked potats... are you
ok with that?
x

. . . .

POTATO

Eventually, in a bid of desperation, I began stripping. You were the first friend I told. I felt ashamed when I took the job and then more ashamed when I sort of liked it. What kind of respectable girl enjoys the feeling of taking off her clothes in front of a paying audience? Slut shaming was a real, consistent trend in 2008. But you were not judgmental, I had told you whilst bracing myself, having decided if you thought it a terrible idea then I would quit. But you got it, you understood (even more so when the money started coming in). You even came to watch a couple of times, I can't remember with whom, maybe that wastrel Nathan, maybe Gabby. Having your support in something I absolutely could not bring up with my family, could not discuss with my other friends, was so key, it made me feel stable in an increasingly disorientating job. Because stripping is disorientating, not just the very late nights you work, but the drinking, the partying, the feeling of not being at work at all but being at a function you cannot leave.

The bubble that becomes all-encompassing in the club, the petty hierarchies of top earners, the sudden dad-like dynamics that develop overnight with the bouncers who see you like a daughter and insist on driving you home, kicking out the guy who was too close, laughing at your jokes. It was a weird, weird world, and to step out of it every night and into your arms was stabilizing.

Often, when I was at the club, you would text me, ask when I was going to be home, if I was going to be hungry, and often when I got home there would be a potato for me, waiting in the microwave. Potatoes were our love language. You need it? I got you. I need it? Don't worry, girl. There's a potato in the oven.

I miss a friendship like that. I miss that undulating yet predictable flow, the safety of a friendship built on bedrock, there was nothing you could do that would jeopardise my love for you, there was nothing I could do that would make you think less of me. It makes me wonder if now that you're dead it continued. If it continues now, if I will always be loved by you because together we built something so steadfast time itself could not corrode it.

There is a power to stripping. I think most people find it demeaning in thought at least, reducing what should be a rare pleasure to a transactional experience. But there is such power in calling the shots, in commanding the room with your clothes off. I had long been a provocative dresser, a lover of short skirts, a lover of transparent shirts with no bra. You had asked once why I dressed the way I did, how it must be exhausting to be ogled, but I told you what I stand by to this day—it felt like control to dress that way. I controlled the eyes on my body instead of most women's reality of being stared at constantly whether we want it or not. Stripping was sort of like that, I controlled it, my sexuality and the power in it was palpable, it was a weapon in the room and, if I wielded it just right, I could get almost anything from these little men, or sometimes (but rarely) women. I looked good and I knew it. I was worth more than they were paying and they knew it. The majority of my time in that career I worked in a club that had strict rules as to distance between dancer and customer, enforced by various cockney men all named Gary, protective of us and ready to fight for whatever honour we held to our chests. Never were we allowed to lean in too close, never was a man allowed to so much as graze our thigh with their hands, there was a power in that too. I was, quite literally, untouchable. I am tall, and in the prerequisite heels I felt like a goddess. My perception of myself, of my beauty, of my faculties changed drastically whilst working there, and I think you knew, Larissa. I think you felt me blossom and that's why you understood my need to do this work, finances aside.

Of course, there were days it was shit, the club was empty or full of arseholes or just a night when I would continue to strike out for no clear reason, perplexed. Days when I was needled by customers thinking they were saving me, asking what I was doing in a place like this as if it was worse than whatever shithole they themselves worked in. There were days my lingerie fit tighter than I remembered and I would get in my head about my weight—a former anorexic is never reformed. There were days when I would call you, crying, just desperate to come home even if I had made only the club's required house fee.

The next day after that type of shift, you would usually do something nice for me. You'd suggest I meet you on your lunch break, you'd bring me back a book you saw in a secondhand shop or a treat from a bakery. Sometimes we would just climb onto our incredibly uncomfortable sofa and watch a movie we'd already seen a thousand times. Of course, sometimes you were too busy for that shit, sometimes I felt ignored but I never felt unloved.

You were good with depressed people. You didn't treat them like fragile china to be handled with care but you gave offerings, little tangible offerings that would hold them over until their minds were a little clearer. You were a good listener. In fact, you still are. I still talk to you as if you are here, I still get that same comfortable silence, as if you are nodding to signal that I may continue.

That time—me stripping, you working in a real three-day-a week job that you actually enjoyed, those days were definitely the wealthiest of our friendship and we still barely had anything to show for it. A flat we were constantly late with the rent on, some vintage dresses, some makeup, too many receipts for too many taxis we shouldn't have been taking. I remember it being fun; I remember it being stressful. I remember that living the majority of my life in the darkness of a strip club when most people I knew were sleeping felt increasingly depressing. When we finally left London for LA, a trip we had convinced one of my regulars to pay for right before I quit stripping for the fourth time, we were so ready for a change of scene. Anything but

London, which you were beginning to truly resent, a feeling that would eventually propel you across the English Channel to Paris. Anything but the same shit, anything but opposite schedules and no time to hang out.

We had a blast, we spent money like we always did, as if someone was right behind us, ready to pry it out of our hands. We met up with other London friends, we went to exclusive parties and discovered the true joy of an LA dive bar, both gritty and glam at the same time. We were lucky and landed on our feet everywhere, it was one of those special trips where both of us were going with it, whatever was suggested we said yes to, whatever was available we did.

Eventually, we ended that trip in the Standard hotel on Sunset and it felt like the right setting for us. It doesn't exist anymore, but back then it was still rock 'n' roll, every night the bar was full, every night we wore something different, ordered eighteen-dollar spaghetti, drank cocktails until someone intervened and started buying them for us (which they always did). We were very beautiful, we were interesting, our accents made us a beacon in any bar. I have no idea how we ordered and paid for so many bottles of champagne. One of our LA days we woke up, had numerous bloody Marys, got cut off by the bartender at eleven thirty in the morning and got in the pool—unheard-of in LA to have a dip in an outdoor pool in December but to us Brits it was practically tropical.

I met Adam on that trip, and that is also remarkable. Remarkable that through the sea of parties and ever-changing faces I found the one face I would stick to for a long time. You knew before I did, I think. You hated every single guy I had ever dated or at the bare minimum you regarded them with a light disdain, but with Adam you were immediately receptive. Not that we spent a lot of time with you on that trip, Adam and I began in a hotel and stayed in a hotel for a while before we realised we liked each other. And when I told you I liked him, liked him liked him, you barely reacted, as if you already knew. You were on his team from the beginning and I am not sure even he knows what a rare feat that is.

shmoo brain

....

Larissa <larry67@xmail.com>
to me

Apr 1, 2012

i would love to speak to you
wish you could go on skype :(

....

Eirinie <eirinieeee@xmail.com>
to Larissa

Apr 1, 2012

I know me too! Planning to get a laptop
soon I hope then I can see your face
whenever I need to!
I miss you so much, I hate being apart
from you!!!

(editors note: my emails to you read
exactly like my emails to A)

....

HI.

It only takes me two glasses of wine to get to the point where I feel like you can hear me. It's very painful, thinking about you and then realising that you're not around. Today I was trying to remember something, if you'd heard of a certain band maybe or what night buses we used to get back from Soho, and I had the stark, almost blinding memory that you are dead.

I want to see you.

I feel as if I now understand people's obsessions with aliens, or ghosts. We need them. We need to believe that it is possible to see, or even just catch a glimpse of the people we loved who are dead. I was on a train back from the airport yesterday and on every platform and in every carriage that whizzed out of view I was searching for you. That stripey shirt. A ripped jean. Your hair. Your skinny legs. Something and anything and everything. I need something concrete; I need to hear you or see you or anything so that this won't feel so final. I want you to hold my hand like you would when we walked down the street. To stand close to me, smiling wide and cocking your head, and say my name the way you did, "Eirins." People rarely said my full name. I rarely introduced myself that way. I was Ree or Rinie or E, but you would full-name me, to the point that I began to do it. I came into my own, I came into Eirinie, and finally, Eirins.

I love you so much.

If this is all there is—building memories and experiences until we are cold in the ground—then I despair even harder. I need to believe that an echo of you drifts around Paris, or paces back and forth in your mother's attic, or hears me when I sing along to the Talking Heads or Brian Jonestown Massacre or the Doors or Slipknot. God, I forgot how much you loved Slipknot.

You were the first person I met who didn't mind contradiction. Every other teen I knew was desperately trying to prove that they loved metal the most, despised everything else. Purists. You didn't give a shit. You loved what you loved and dared people to challenge you on it. It gave me the confidence to be me, instead of what I thought I should be.

I remember once when we were teens at a party, I teased you when you asked a question about something commonplace, something most people knew. I teased you because I was trying to be cool, trying to seem cynical and bored. You called me on it. You said, "How do you know the things you know? Because you asked somebody." And it shut me up and I felt awful but then later on I understood a whole new way of viewing people: not naive, not idiots, just people who hadn't asked the right question yet.

You were a mentor but at the same time, I protected you. I was your baby sister but also your longtime love and kindred. You taught me, I taught you. I was poor, you gave me money. You were desperate to leave London, I got us plane tickets to LA.

Sitting around the pool at the Standard on Sunset, we were broke beyond belief, forlorn and hungry, unsure of how we would even get to the airport without money to pay for the cab, when two young men appeared on the balcony above us. Bolstered by your confidence in me, I smiled, waved them down and before we knew it, two French men were offering us roles in a music video if we would just stay. They paid for us to change our flights, paid for us to stay another week (!) at the Standard. As a mother and an actual adult woman I'm now chilled to the bone by this story, thinking how they could have murdered and discarded our bodies in the Death Valley canyons that we drove to with them, how we could have been drugged and raped or fallen victim to any number of atrocities that happen to young women on a daily basis. But none of this occurred. We were safe, they fed us and bought our drinks and paid for our room service (which we absolutely rinsed with late-night spaghetti and bottles of champagne). They didn't hit on us, in fact one of their girlfriends came out from Paris to DJ at the hotel. I'm sure she was absolutely thrilled to see us, loud and leggy and far too comfortable with her man. We made no money but we partied like it was the last time, I facilitated so much with the confidence you instilled in me. You made me feel beautiful and reckless, I was Nancy I was Courtney I was Poly Styrene I was Grace Jones I felt the sex the minute we walked into a room together.

Midway through this bonus week in LA, this unexpected patronage, our friend Gemma stepped onto our hotel room balcony. Gemma was anything but a wallflower, a gorgeous blonde little thing possessing the boldness of beautiful white women everywhere, and she began cackling out in the dark. You and I couldn't fathom whose ear she was chewing off and so we stepped out too and who was there on his adjoining balcony but Adam. He looked at me, I looked at him. I knew I would sleep with him in that exact instant. I said, "Hi, I'm Eirinie but you'll never remember that." He said "Oh I'll remember" with a confidence that I knew meant he wouldn't.

Later, when he slipped a note under our door asking us all to have a drink and Gemma and I bickered about who he really wanted to have a drink with, you nudged me down to the hotel bar with some sort of psychic premonition. And the rest, as they say, is history.

You were my nudger. The forcer of my hand, the engine. So much of my story starts with a whisper of faith from you. I worry now that I have lost that, that I cannot re-create that on my own, that without your blind and unwavering optimism in my skills I will wither into a hopeless raisin.

Since you died I have been writing a lot more. It is ironic that my first book, my most precious body of work, came out of your death. You, my most fervent champion of my writing. Something like poppies growing on graves, something like a diamond being made out of ashes. A steady stream has poured out onto the page. I often wonder, in my deep grieving madness, if it isn't your hands at the keyboard, steady and certain, editing my words into something cohesive, something beautiful and something true.

I am grateful for everything I ever shared with you, but it wasn't enough. I want more of you, I want to watch *Grey's Anatomy* with you and get dressed up for cocktails but end up staying home with you, I want to share an Oyster card fare with you and bunk off work with you and get drunk with you.

I miss you in a way I'm not sure I've ever missed anyone. I miss you like I can't get you back.

Larissa <larry67@xmail.com>   Nov 13, 2009
to me

o dearies
just spilt red wine on my job seekers
allowance form i have to hand in every
week! think that will be ok!?

hahahahaha x

HAMSTER

There was a day, back in oh, 2011 or 2012, when you called me in a panic. You couldn't clearly tell me what was wrong over the phone, you were frantic, out in our garden, refusing to go in the house. I can't remember where I was, somewhere far though, maybe a casting or something, but when I got this call I headed for the Tube, rushing to get home. You kept saying you couldn't get ahold of Charlie. You seemed angry with her. I remember wondering if she had had a date over who had become aggressive or stolen shit. I remember running through possibilities as I changed tubes for the Northern line, jumped off at East Finchley, half-trotted half-ran up Southern Road to our flat.

I found you in the garden as promised, you had been comforted by our downstairs neighbours, who had made you tea, had you sit down. I personally thought the husband of that older couple was a little too fascinated by us, but you disagreed when I suggested that. Anyway, there you were, fuming in the backyard, smoking a cig.

You had calmed down enough to tell me what was wrong. Charlie had forgotten to close her hamster cage properly and it had gotten out and startled you as you were in the kitchen cleaning. You told this story with a frantic energy and I kept waiting for the part where I was supposed to join you in your anger.

A hamster.

Had been witnessed by you.

In the kitchen.

That was it. That was the panic. I tried not to laugh. I knew you hated animals, particularly rodents. You didn't think there was anything cute about puppies, you thought kittens were gross, but rodents, no. Rodents you would kill. Charlie's hamster had no idea how lucky it was.

I went inside to find the thing but couldn't, and by that stage Charlie had received your voicemail and hurried home, wondering where the fire was. Charlie was, and is, a sweet person who has a strong desire not to disappoint anyone, and so to come home to an angry Larissa (formidable at any time but when aimed right, terrifying) and a lost hamster was almost too much for her.

She located the creature, shut it in its cage, promised it would never happen again to an incredibly surly you. She probably endured a week of silent treatment. I did my best to keep the peace but I probably sided with you, which was always the wise move.

You were such a particular person, there was no room for error with you. In some ways I found this refreshing. I am a person who likes rules, tell me the rules and I will follow them gladly, happy for the guidance and structure. In other ways your idiosyncrasies sometimes made for narrow perimeters. You were flexible with some people; some were allowed to make mistakes. I, for example, managed to escape your wrath on multiple occasions purely because you knew that my aim was true and if I offended your sensibilities it was usually an honest mistake.

The things I loved most about you, the things I treasure still, are things that often made you impossible to deal with. That day with the hamster I dropped everything to help you, and I am not sure you said thank you. It was often like this, if I am honest, a battle to stay within the lines you had drawn for life, and a thankless one at that. Your moods could fluctuate at the drop of a hat and it wasn't always clear why, I could read them well because my mother was the same, it was better to be ready to bend and accommodate than to demand to know what was wrong. And so often, I fear, I sacrificed myself for you, for your comfort.

And I think that is where the guilt I feel about your death comes from. Towards what we now know was the end of your life, that last year or two, I started to put my foot down with you, I became less dependent on your approval, I saw myself fully formed without you, I saw that you needed me more than I needed you and so I pulled away. I wouldn't blindly send you money, I wouldn't drop everything to have a bitch with you about someone we once knew. I had a life, a child, a husband, I thought loftily. I don't have time for this shit.

Knowing what I know now, you needing me more was exactly the reason I should have had time, should have made time. You needed me but I pulled away. I pulled so far that when you died, I had to jog to get back into place, I had to write a eulogy for your funeral that would cement me in the role I had always been in, up until recently.

I wish I had made time.

Does that mean I killed you? Does that mean that I am responsible, that I partly carry the blame for what happened to you? No. I don't think so. You knew I was there, and you also, I am sure, knew the exact combination of words you could have said to make me look up, snap to it, pay attention. You didn't reach out and neither did I. If that is stubborn then I inherited it from you. I made my own rules and perimeters. I didn't move them for anyone and it wasn't until you died that I realised that I could have helped yours come down a long time ago.

Larissa <larry67@xmail.com>   Feb 7, 2013,
to me   4:10 AM

Oh happy bday to a. How old is he now?
Broc and mash! We really are old now!!!!
Yikes!!! Especially as that sounds delic
to me! Even the vegetarian part! Lol
Dude are you modeling in sf now??
The agency will let you? ThTs bloody
excellent! How's the planning going? Yeh
it's approaching soon! How fun!
Will it be boiling hot or just warm? Or
neither?!!!
I really wish I could afford a bloody
plane ticket to America…
Oh you're def doin Paris?! That's fun! Yeh
of course I know all the good places to
go, I live here now!!!
When are you going to London??? I'm going
to make you come visit me this time, no
excuses
What you doing today?
I'm going to the ballet this eve but first
I must find some coffee. Being caffeinated
regularly is like breathing in Paris. You
know it's only 2€ for coffee maybe 3€ in
posh places so its actually affordable. I
went to Starbucks yesterday and nearly
went my pants when I was charge a fiver.
Fucking daylight robbery I tell you!!
Couldn't believe it! I had forgotten that
Starbucks was so expensive..
And on that note ill go and be a granny
elsewhere
Xxxx

I THINK THAT

I think that, the thing is, the thing is, the thing is . . . none of us, not the grieving, not the people watching the grieving ones, want to believe that life can change in a way that is beyond our control. To acknowledge that grief and mourning last long after the black clothes are changed, long after the weeds grow in on the grave, long after we no longer cry at the sound of their name, would be to acknowledge that something has permanently shifted. We are no longer who we were because if we were, we wouldn't still be sad, we would have forgotten entirely the events that transpired when we lost our person. But these things never go away, and so that means a permanent change has occurred. That is scary for people because it signifies that we cannot control what we kid ourselves every day into thinking we can.

And that's probably why I so often find my mind drifting to death and corpses and the endless bleak possibilities my life holds, because I now know. I've seen it, firsthand, this unpredictability. The curtain has been torn away and I see the man behind it. No one is afforded anything, no amount of prayer or hope can keep us from what will happen, what could happen.

I don't mean this to be macabre but to most it will be because it is looking directly into the face of a truth we'd rather not have acknowledged. But really, what a gift! What a gift not to live every day as if it is a given, what a gift to know that when you reach over to hold your spouse's hand, when you feel their pulse and have them squeeze back in that old familiar way, this small insignificance is It. This is the Thing. These little moments are what make up the joy, the little moments I had with Larissa are all I have of her now and so really, they were the only important things all along. Not the fretting over bills, not the brief but fiery disagreements, not the hidden secrets, but the times when a moment of silence passed between us, a knowing smile across a room, an unexpected hug. These are the things. And so now I know, if I treasure these little items scattered throughout my life then I shall find solace at the moment of my death because my god, I have so many moments of beauty.

Most of my friends are waiting for some kind of special day when happiness will abound: if I can just lose the weight, if I can just move to a bigger place, if I can just get this job, then everything will be good and I'll be in a Good Place. We focus on the big goals because the small shit isn't as exciting, doesn't have the longevity. And when we reach the goal we are inevitably depressed because the moment has come but the happiness has not. I feel as if my sadness over Larry's death is inextricably tied to this concept. I keep expecting to wake up one day and be on the other side of it all. Like in the movies. Rested, rejuvenated, ready to smile, rejoin society without the fear of unpredictable tears. It's just out there on the horizon, this fabled recovery, I just need to

I just need to

I just need to

I just need to

The days I let go of this notion are better. The pressure seems lower, the hurdles are smaller. I have somehow, against all odds, reached a place where my grief and I are friends. I can hold hands with it, I can have frank discussions and I can also have some space from it. Maybe "friends" is wrong, more like "flatmates." I live with it now and we are both on an unbreakable lease, I understand that it is going nowhere, I'll have to put up with the used milk and unbought toilet paper, I'll have to deal with the pain and inconvenience of it in order to reach that harmonious coexisting.

The threads are the thing, not the patchwork bits of cloth but the tiny, sometimes easy-to-miss threads that hold those parts together. The thrill of house hunting—opening a door, imagining what type of person you'd be in each new place—is greater than the eventual purchase of the home and realisation of its flaws. The moments your daughter forces you to colour with her, even though you have ten thousand other things to do, and you're resentful for the first five minutes until you realise you've been blissfully scribbling in a content calm with your child, a memory she will most definitely forget. It is these in-between bits I look for now, the inconsequential and the dull. Those are the memories I cherish.

Eirinie <eirinieeee@xmail.com>   May 13, 2011
to Larissa

did you comb your hair on the sofa last
night? Either that or youre going bald!
Was quite a job to get them all!
Im baking more cookies!

Larissa <larry67@xmail.com>   May 13, 2011
to me

LOOOOOLLL
Yes, was brushing. Soz x

C H A P T E R 2 1

HERITAGE

Larissa and I were similar but the similarities that strike home the most now for me are the foundational ones, the fires in which we were forged. The eldest daughters of single mothers, we both had younger brothers who, in the shadow of their gleaming elder sisters, could only seem troublesome, out-of-control boys who needed their fathers. We both excelled at English literature, at school in general, me with a little more effort than her, she with a nonchalance she would carry into adulthood.

There was so much for us to understand about each other and maybe that helped. She was the first (and for a long time, only) person I spoke to about my father, that estranged lanky Jamaican I pined for in a way I somehow convinced myself was ambivalence. She never spoke of hers, save a couple of times when we were drunk, or curled in bed in that exclusive little duvet bundle impenetrable to anyone else. I have nothing to say about her father, I do not know him and the little tastes of him I got have been swallowed like a secret poison. So much was common ground.

Perhaps that was the thing, the X factor over which our friends marveled. Perhaps that's what Maddy meant when she said I was closest to her. Because we were so alike in the most fundamental, the most nurture-versus-nature of ways. It's bizarre to think of those two girls, lost and defiant and smarter than most, and how different their lives became. I got married at twenty-five, pregnant at twenty-eight, desperate in that eldest daughter's way to build the perfect family unit I had craved since my parents' divorce. She was different, a long love in Pierre, yes, but after and before it was almost dizzying the rate at which she would fall in love with a beauty. I am not saying that one path is better than the other, not advocating for marriage or any of its perceived stabilities as the answer, but we suddenly diverged and that was the beginning of a different chapter of friendship. I always was the crowd-pleaser. I struggle with the knowledge of disappointing people, I have trod this path of goody two-shoes (with the occasional gaffes) so carefully and somehow it has walked me into a stable and loving relationship, a child I adore. Larissa did nothing for anyone, she put her needs and desires before almost everything else, and in doing so lived in an honest way.

Why did Larissa do the things she did? Party and love and lust after and dazzle every person she encountered? Perhaps because for Larissa the joy of life was in the moment, the very fabric of the moment. Not in the anticipation, although she often said she preferred the act of getting ready to the letdown of a disappointing party. But for Larissa it was now, right fucking now and if she couldn't feel it, that sense of nothing else existing except the moment she was in, then she was out.

She gave me so much and lately, one gift I think of often that I didn't always think of before was the gift of Black family. Raised by a blonde, white mother, with very few, inaccessible little ties to my father's island, I struggled. Being light-skinned in the UK was like a special in-between zone. You are "other," for sure, but the door is opened for you before it would ever be opened for someone darker. As a teen I rarely wore my hair natural because that felt like amplifying something I hadn't acknowledged, something I wanted distance from. Living in America as a light-skinned person is very different, I am definitively Black here and I wonder how long it would have taken for me to feel that back home. I believe that the dissonance I felt between my Blackness and myself was very much to do with the absence of my father. If he had helped raise me how could there be any question about who I am and where I am from? I don't think I really recognised the Blackness in me until quite late. I mean, I knew I was brown, but I don't think I saw that I was truly a part of the Black experience for a while. When I met Larry one of the first things she did was invite me to stay at her house, where I met her mother, where I met her brother. Eventually, on a summer break from the (very white) boarding school in which I was now enrolled, I stayed for the long haul, long enough for my mother to send her mother money to feed and house me. Larissa's mother is not a woman of fluffy maternal sentiments. She is practical and fearless and driven. And so, I was simply accepted as one of the family. A plate was laid for me, my laundry was folded on my bed just as Larry's was on hers, her brother teased me like he teased his sister. It was such a complete unspoken absorption that I barely noticed it, and it is only now I can see what a well-timed gift this was for me.

I think I never felt I could lay a claim on the Black part of me as I knew almost nothing about it, felt too embarrassed to ask. Shouldn't I know already? It was only with Larissa that I felt that part unfurl like a new leaf, a realisation that my Blackness was whatever I was, it was not definable by trends or accents or clothes. Later, a move to America in which black and white feels so much more capital-B Black and capital-W White than it does in the UK, particularly for a mixed-heritage woman. Racism in the UK for me was quiet, discreet, a bee sting. You don't notice it at first, a small needle in your side as someone tells you how well-spoken you are and then later it swells and pulses with pain and you realise how much damage it has done. In the US racism is a gunshot, loud and immediate, like the word "nigger" being yelled at you in the park, a man mimicking a monkey at you as you walk down the street with your husband. With that sort of explosive racism you reckon with it much more in real time. Moving to America made me realise how indistinguishable I am from my heritage even when I know so little about it, and if knowing so little was shameful to me, then that was something I had to reckon with too. To stand in my Blackness became imperative to me, a journey that started with being invited into the Broadfield Road house, that started with being welcomed into Larissa's family.

We started in roughly the same spot, Larissa and I. And yet we ended up in such different places. I was nervous to tell her I was pregnant, what would she think of me? That I was pedestrian and basic and not the person she thought I was (and I hoped I was) at all?

I got married young to the rock star, Larry dated different variations of the same rock 'n' roll guy on and off, she was in Paris (chic and sophisticated and worldly), I was in California (bohemian and casual and slow-paced).

Even Larissa's death. As horrid as it was, as painful as it is to think of, that was rock 'n' roll. No one can take that from her. She died beautiful and young and full of untapped potential and what am I? A mother? I followed the rules and played the game and lucky lucky lucky for me I am mostly happy in the life I found for myself, so far removed from the periodic poverty and the loneliness and the uncertainty. It is dark to think of it this way, macabre and simplistic, and yet I know this would have brought her some joy. Larry got what we all wanted—beauty, immortality, the dramatic flourish of the final curtain, no encore baby, that's all folks.

Larissa <larry67@xmail.com>   Mar 15, 2010
to me

Dam, casting for negro hair tomorrow!!
I actuatlly hav a chance for that hair
job!! But I'm working in publishers. Go
and make mother proud! One of us should
get it at least!! Make sure your curly
mccurlson tho ;)
Xxxx

YOUR FACE

J onny Santos, our friend from New York, sent me a bunch of photos and videos from our time in Brooklyn in 2008–2009. I scrolled through, mostly loving it, mostly being reminded of all the weirdos we met, all the bars we went to, all the stupid in-jokes that are no funnier now than they were then but still I laugh. And then I found one video. It is short, it is you and Jonny at brunch somewhere in Williamsburg, the camera is framed steadily on you, and you fluctuate between pretending nothing is happening and pouting about him filming you.

You are candid and I was immediately reminded of all those tiny idiosyncrasies that made you so effervescent, so difficult to describe with words. Your big doe eyes, batting your lashes in frustration, swatting at Jonny, saying his name with that fond annoyance that was so particular to you. You have mosquito bites, you tell him, they itch so bad you want to scratch them off—here you emphasise the word "off," another signature move, another

little tic of yours. You mime the action, as if you really could tear
your own skin off, you laugh. It is a short video. It is really short,
maybe a minute and a half and yet it broke my heart clean in two.
I had been waiting to watch those videos, waiting for a day I felt
strong and not already in a pit of despair about losing you. But
the video broke me in a way I was not expecting and suddenly
the tears came and I couldn't quell them, I could not stop sobbing,
it was the most I have ever cried, the amount of liquid felt comi-
cal. Like a manga cartoon, little rivers streaming down my cheeks,
soaking the neck of my shirt.

There is another video, only one other although I wish for
more the way a glutton wishes for punishment. It is the same scene,
the table at brunch but this time you take the camera, film Jonny,
ask the waitress if she'd like to be filmed. You cannot be seen, just
your voice and it is like looking through your eyes, it is briefly
(for it is brief) sci-fi, like I have stepped inside your skin, like you
finally tore it off and let me in.

I love this video too, although it makes me cry less. It is a
wish, granted. I have spent the last two years since you died wondering what the fuck you were thinking, reconstructing your final thoughts and sights and sounds in my head, trying to get into
yours. And suddenly, for approximately a minute and ten seconds,
I make it. Here I am. It is just as beautiful as I thought it would be.
And perhaps, if I am honest, I have been craving being inside your
magical head for longer than two years. If I am honest you have
been the one person who has been inimitable and yet the one I have
most desired to be like.

You were confident of yourself in a way that so few people are, at least not until deep into later life. You were gorgeous in an easy, effortless way, not that you didn't try with your appearance but that you could be in a designer dress and be stunning, a leather jacket and be stunning, your pj's and your hair wrapped and be stunning.

I never really understood why you didn't book more as a model. For sure you were a crappy model in that you rarely went to castings, were often late for shoots, but you were undeniably beautiful in an ethereal, queenly way. I think you were ahead of your time; I think back then the industry didn't have time for your beauty, there was one dark-skinned Black girl allowed through the door at a time and Sonja Wanda beat you to it. Even though Sonja Wanda often had blue contacts in and weave back then, straddling the line between an Afro idea of beauty and an Anglo one. You didn't look alike, not really, and yet that was the reason cited for not booking work for a long time—they already booked Sonja, Sonja did that campaign last year so now they're going for a different look. And even Sonja, with all of her success and fortune, didn't book what her white peers did. She was still the outlier, still the model you booked if you were feeling spicy, a little diversity to brighten up your highly Caucasian runway.

Maybe you knew that, knew the limits imposed upon you as a dark-skinned Black model, maybe that's why sometimes it felt as if you didn't give a shit. Maybe you knew they didn't and so you didn't. I know that I as a light-skinned, loose-curled model booked more stuff because I was and am considered more palatable, the closest many brands still feel they can come to Blackness, a toe dipped in the water, the feeling of a pat on the back as if to say, we did it. We got a Black. That'll do, pig. That'll do.

But neither of us booked that much. Both of us heard "We already have a Black model on this job" several million times. In our emails to each other we barely even register disgust at the industry, when we talked it was with a knowing, jaded sigh. I still sigh, sometimes.

What a beauty you were. There is no other word for it. A face that made people stop and stare, and then that brain . . . that brain. It held so much knowledge, you held your own with the smartest people we met, and yet you were never too proud to say you didn't know something. You weren't pretentious with what you knew, you didn't talk down to people who didn't know the same shit as you. It was so refreshing. You were like no other girl in London, on the planet, and people told you this frequently.

poopoohead

 Larissa <larry67@xmail.com>
to me

Aug 13, 2016,
12:42 PM

so proud of you poo
working in NY thats really amazing youre
so great
i just dreamed of you it was insane you
were dressed like lauren bacall and you
invited me into your beautiful mansion you
looked so beautiful!!!
i SOO need to see u poohead
tell me how was new york film thing?
also OMG about nick is he OK? let me know
about that
love u soo much and well done
sorry for writing so late !!! xxxx
also can u write me a leter or send me
something in the mail i never get anything only pierre and we have this really
nice mailbox and i get jealous! feel free
to send things to like a new dress or a
cheque ;)

ALL RIGHT
HERE'S THE DEAL

A ll right here's the deal, Larry.

Here's the fucking deal. I am going to go to a medium for the first time in my life, I am going to suspend my disbelief for a little while and go sit with a woman who will probably be wearing a lot of turquoise, probably just make an educated guess what my reasons were for being there. I will go in, I will pay money, I will believe for the twenty minutes or however long a psychic reading takes, and I will wait. And here's where you come in. You will materialise. That's the deal. I'm meeting you in the middle, I am doing something I never thought I would in order to see if you'll meet me halfway.

You were never really a halfway girl, so why that would change now you're dead I have no idea, but maybe, maybe if you really did visit Pierre in that dream he described, maybe you'll come to me too. All you have to do is show up. I am not expecting full-body apparitions, just something, even a glimmer of something.

One of the things I love most about you, and yes, I use the present tense because my god I still actively love it, was your inability to do anything you didn't want to do. You were so specific and so stubborn in your specificity. Everyone getting ready for a night out, makeup on, heels on, cab called but suddenly you didn't want to go? You just . . . wouldn't go. You wouldn't force yourself to take part in something you knew to be a waste of time, somehow you had this deep, innate knowledge of yourself and what you expected from life and you wouldn't bypass it for anyone. Not even me. On numerous occasions I had absolutely begged you to come to some party or some club or some event, hiding my anger, dolled up and ready for a drink, begged you to come if only for an hour, I'd pay your cab home I'd buy you a drink I'd . . . I'd . . . you could never be swayed once you had decided. Nope. Wasn't worth it. You'd take off your makeup, wrap your hair, pj's on, *SATC* on before I was out the door. And you know what? You were always, always infuriatingly right. How did you know? How did you sense that it would be shit music or over-priced cocktails or awful people or a long wait for nothing?

I wonder now if that's true, if you really had some gift for knowing when a party was going to be shit or if once you had proclaimed something to be a disappointment, I could no longer see a point to it. Maybe your opinions coloured my worldview so much that I would make the parties terrible all by myself.

Maybe you died at thirty-two because you knew, some-fucking-how, that it wouldn't get much better. That's a depressing thought maybe, but it could also be bolstering. It could also be that you just knew when to leave. I don't know. Searching for meaning in the most meaningless event in our lives feels a little stupid but I still search. I still want to solve the mystery even if mysteries are, by nature, supposed to remain that way. If it were solvable it wouldn't be a mystery anymore.

I never really understood why people went to mediums, it seemed so transparent, so clearly a scam that I pitied them. I thought they were desperate, I thought they were gullible, I thought they were crappy with money. And now here I am, bargaining with a ghost I can't even see, whose presence I can't even feel. I am not sure what to expect. A table shake? A butterfly? A cold feeling on a hot day? What would be your style? You'd be scoffing at me for sure, you'd think I was hilarious, you'd be saying, "Eirins! How much did this cost? How much?! Yeah, you could have gotten a bottle of champs for that, I'd be way more likely to show up for champs!"

I suppose when I think about it, I am desperate . . . The shoe fits. So, I will try it on, I will step into a realm of thinking I previously would have scoffed at. Unlike you, I am willing to go to the party, to see what it is like.

I want to lay out a Ouija board, surround it with crystals and personal items, whatever you do with Ouija boards (I dunno because my mother would never have allowed such Satanism into her home), I would have done what was necessary to open that portal. The experts, the people who know about these things, the occult and all that (my aunt Philena, for example) would tell me that you cannot control such a portal. You cannot only allow the one spirit in that you desire, once the door is open it is open to all. You know not what you are inviting.

To me, this is not a deterrent. To me, a person starved of my loved one, parched for her and desperate, I say fling that door open wide. Whoever comes, comes. I'll take the chance just to see her.

It is with this in mind that I have booked my appointment with the psychic. I want to be taken in. Tell me what I need to hear, I'll say as I sit down in the chair. I don't care. I need to feel something, I need to feel her close even if it is just smoke and mirrors.

Perhaps, if I am lucky, I will smell her one last time, like how stroke victims smell burning toast right before they succumb. I'll smell her and then I will be somewhere else, with her, briefly so briefly but just long enough to feel a kinship again. I'll pay what needs to paid for that. I'll risk it all.

Now I understand why so many people go to mediums and dust off their Ouija boards or light their candles and hope for a miracle, spells and sorcery. It is the desperation. The fear that the door has been closed behind them and no amount of pounding will open it. How thick is this door and when will it open for me? I don't need to go through exactly, I just need it to open like in horror movies, creaking, revealing whatever is beyond, but most important, a glimpse of Larissa, a glimpse of life beyond death, a glimpse that means I am not the sole survivor of this friendship. Give me death. Show me it. I am not afraid; I am steeled and ready.

The psychic I finally go to describes you in the afterlife in a bucolic field, surrounded by animals. I cannot think of anything you'd despise more. Hay fever? Creatures? There's no way. I tell the medium this, breaking my rule about oversharing, and she quickly course-corrects, tells me you had been given the choice to live your life over again or not, and you had chosen not. And so picking wildflowers had been your fate. I laugh inwardly. There is no way your afterlife is a field full of bunnies and cats and woodland critters. Surely a bar with a sticky floor, loud music, cute androgyny everywhere. But maybe the medium was right. Maybe you'd done that for so long, maybe that was so old hat that the afterlife had granted you a taste of something new, a taste of a life you never even thought of for yourself. Maybe that was part of the healing, maybe that was part of your journey. If so, I hope I see that field one day, I hope I lie in the grass and look up at the sky with you, I am not sure we ever did that in real life.

The psychic also tells me that we had met before, Larissa and I. We were soul sisters; we had met and would keep on meeting. What a joyous thought, what a pearl of hope to press into my grasping hand. She says that in our past lives we had been wives to the same man, and had found sisterhood in that, which makes so much sense because we would have been great bitchy little wives to some poor medieval fool.

And then the psychic cocks her head to the side and says, someone is a teacher.

She was, I reply. Larissa was my teacher.

But the psychic shakes her head and tells me that no, it is me. I am the teacher.

Larissa <larry67@xmail.com>   Mar 1, 2012
to me

████ is leaving today – u have no idea
how happy i am to be alone
again. no idea. having freinds is
oveeratted!!!

Larissa <larry67@xmail.com>   Mar 1, 2012
to me

apart from u shmoo shmoo!!!
i cant believe ive ever been angry wiith u
in my life u are actual
gold dust – heaven sent compared to
everone else on earth!!!
everything smells of poo when your not
here poo head!!

Eirinie <eirinieeee@xmail.com>   Mar 1, 2012
to Larissa

Oh shmoomalates that was almost a sonnet!

YOUR SMELL

Since Larissa died, whenever I get the chance to hug Maddy or Natalia, the hug feels deeper. It is a hug that is proxy for so many things—for the sorrow we all feel, because I am sorry for their loss and they are sorry for mine. A hug for the person we really want to be hugging. It isn't as good as hugging Larissa, obviously, but there is something about our combined sadnesses that makes us feel like something is shared, that we are no longer alone in this loss.

When Larissa was alive, she gave great hugs. She would rock you side to side with her, as if she were so happy to see you that she couldn't contain her joy. She smelt amazing, too. Her hair smelt like her products, her perfume. When I got a bag of her things after she died, I opened it excitedly. I expected to smell her, I expected to be catapulted back into our friendship. Time travelling on scent—Larissa, alive again for a moment. But in reality, she was dead for a long time before I got hold of her things. If I had

lived closer I would have travelled to Paris, joined with Simon and
Natalia and Pierre in disassembling her apartment, boxing things,
sorting through what would go to her mother and what would
be divided amongst her friends. I would have had first choice,
probably. I would have been able to find the gems amongst all her
things that held the memories to which I wanted to cling. But instead, I was sent a few bits of clothing, a few pieces of jewelry that,
quite honestly, meant nothing to me. The books that I had actually
wanted were given to Larissa's mum, as she had plans of starting a
library in her name in her village in Ghana, and how could I say no
to that idea? How could I selfishly state that no, in fact, I wanted
her Baldwins and her Sartres. I wanted to see her handwriting in
the margins, I wanted to read her mind as I read them, as if she
were there reading over my shoulder, as if we were once more
discussing literature together. Me with my half-formed, amateur-
hour commentary, her with comparisons and quotes and expertly
viewed observations, deftly turning my head to a completely different theme within whatever book, making me pick up the book
again, reread until I could see what she was seeing.

Instead, I got a plastic bag with three items of clothing. I don't
remember the specific articles off the top of my head and something in me prevents me from reopening it, being confronted with
the fact that the clothes are just fucking clothes now. There is nothing to them. They are not special or even unique. I cannot even
remember seeing her in them.

Most of all they smell nothing like her, they smell like nothing. I was sure the bag would open and she would pop up, fully

formed. But it's just a bag. A bag that now sits in my attic, a bag within a plastic box, waiting for some time when I feel strong enough to open it again. Maybe I will show my daughters. Maybe I will wear something. Maybe, against all odds, the scent will have returned and we will be reunited, clinging to empty clothes that are full of her.

It reminds me of when my grandmother died and I grabbed a handful of things from her room, like someone grabbing their valuables as a fire swiftly engulfs their home, plucking at items with impunity, unsure of what is most important, what they'll need. I grabbed so many things that weren't important to her at all, things that didn't hold any echo of her but I hoped they did, I held them up to my face like a seashell, hoping to hear the ocean. Perhaps soon I can go back to London, back to her tiny little room in Enfield, perhaps Larissa's mother will let me go through her things and find some treasures, something that speaks to me more than the few items with which I am burdened. Burdened because I cannot throw them out, and I cannot look at them. They are relics of absolutely nothing yet I am attached, albatrosses at my neck.

If I had something that meant something to me or to her, perhaps I could feel close to her. As of now I have nothing except my writing to draw her out from the ether, summon her beside me.

Love u poo

. . . .

L **Larissa** <larry67@xmail.com>   Feb 10, 2016,
to me   1:26 AM

I write u emails in my head all the time
i miss u amd thi k about how i can get to
the states to see you! How was LA did u
get any jobx?

Love u popoxxxxx

. . . .

INVISIBLE GRIEF

I recently asked a bunch of people on Instagram what they wish they could say to the loved ones they lost.

I was overwhelmed by the response. Not just the content but also the sheer volume of people, seemingly regular people who post meals they've made, trips they've taken, sunsets they've seen, and yet are haunted by the loss of a loved one and the many things that death left unspoken. They walk among us, these grieving people. Grieving still after years, struggling to put to rest the questions they have for their dead.

It isn't this small little contingency of bereft people that eventually get up, dust themselves off, and rejoin the living, no. They are right here next to us, followed by the specters of their beloveds, the specters of the words they never got to utter. And all the things left unsaid they wish they could say?

Are you proud of me?

Did I do enough for you?

Were you in pain at the end?

Were you happy when you were with us?

So much of grief is the sudden chasm between the things we wish
we had said or asked or acknowledged and what we'd actually
done. All those dead people. They left us without answers and so
now we drag them around, the shadows of them, and ask of them
questions they will never respond to.

A few answers on Instagram were brief, but most were long,
volunteering far more information about their beloved people than
they might have if it were not for the anonymity of the forum,
or perhaps the casual nature of an Instagram question box. I saw
pictures of grandmas and best friends and siblings and I tried to
respond to every single one because I know that feeling, that anx-
ious need to have someone else remember with you, convince you
you're not just seeing things. It's in our nature really, to want other
people to love our loves with us. So why do grieving people so often feel as if they must keep this loss and therefore their loves quiet?
As if no one must know that they are hurting and that they want
us to see their hurt. What has our culture done to our ability to ex-
press raw and often uncomfortable emotion? And how do we undo
it? How do we publicly acknowledge these apparitions of our past?

Did you know how much I loved you?

Is there peace wherever you went?

Do you know how sorry I am?

You did so much for us and I never told you, how can I tell you?

What are we supposed to do with these questions? Because even though for most of them we can assume the answers, we cannot hear them and we so need to hear them. I think about that rule about ghosts. The one that all ghost enthusiasts know—if you confront the ghost, acknowledge it, give it permission to leave, it will do so and you will be left in peace. But what if you can't confront it? What if you're not there yet? What if to look at your perceived failures, the way you think you failed that person who died, is too much? What if you think it will kill you, tether them to this world more firmly, flesh them out in a way you do not want, make them vengeful? What then? You're left with a haunting that may follow you to the end.

I used to think I was a morning writer. I still kid myself that I am. I wake up, I make tea or coffee, put on some lo-fi instrumental noise, and sit at my actual desk in my actual office and open my laptop. Sometimes I write a page or two and then my gaze drifts out the window to the beautiful California day outside. But lately I've noticed I write more in the dark.

In the daytime everything is as it should be, we can see the outlines of things clearly, everyone knows nothing haunts you in daylight. We are the people we are trying to be in the daylight, we know our roles and our lines and we know how to look like we know what we are doing. But in the gloom of the night suddenly things jump out from the darkness, we wonder if what we thought was a lamp is actually a person, leaning towards us, waiting for us to notice. There is no distinguishable difference between our hand in the dark and the dark itself. Things blur.

Right now, I am writing this in the Notes app of my iPhone, my husband asleep beside me. Something about the darkness brings me clarity, makes me see things I can't in the daytime. Maybe there was that certain type of darkness in the Instagram DMs, something similar to this dark room I am in, that made the supernatural feel closer, made that boundary between the past and present seem a little thinner, as if maybe if we lie still enough and think hard enough a little ghost hand will reach out of the gloom and touch our shoulder, not to scare us but to let us know that they are close. We are not alone.

Is it enough, the way I am remembering you?

Do you know how often I think of you?

Was your life fulfilling?

Why didn't you tell me?

Larissa <larry67@xmail.com>   Jul 11, 2009
to me

    nick says its raining in brighton and its
    grim... so is ther a party cuz ill invite
    him oui??! decided on a black dress! black
    tights you know how we roll x x x x

SHE DID NOT
KILL HERSELF

Who is to say that Larissa's life was any less full than it could have been? People live into their nineties and have less to say for their time on this Earth than Larissa could have at the end of her life. Can you mourn that sort of joie de vivre, that fullness and vibrancy and time just busting at the seams with emotion and adventure and thoughts? Does the length of her life detract from her life itself, such as it was? I say no. I say her time here was spent in abundance, moment to moment, a twenty here meant a bottle of wine there, a night out was glittering with possibility, a night in was unapologetically full of her favourite things. She lived a life that was exactly by her terms. I'd argue the only thing she ever did without consenting fully was dying. That she didn't expect, no matter what her fair-weather friends I had never heard of until the funeral may say. She did not kill herself. This I know because I know my Larissa, our Larissa. I know her staunch limitations, I know where the line would have been crossed. She would never have committed suicide, not during the week her cherished mother was due for a visit, there is no way. Her mother was so beloved; Larry would never have done anything to cause such overt harm as to allow her to be present for her death.

She would never have been caught naked, either. Larissa was, despite all her rock 'n' roll trappings, a prude, modest and surprisingly traditional. It wasn't her style to be an exhibitionist. She would not have killed herself whilst she was naked. That would not have been her way.

If she was to kill herself she would have dressed, done it on a bridge maybe, a train platform. Something quick, something solitary. A bath, naked, as her mother travelled from London to Paris to see her? It is out of the question.

Perhaps one needs to know the intricacies of Larissa in order to understand that fundamental impossibility. It is why, at her wake, I wanted to punch the one man who was saying, with an authority not given to him by me or anyone who truly knew Larry, that she killed herself, he was sure of it. I don't know why I didn't slap him or chastise him; I regret that now and given the opportunity to see him again I would gladly tell him how wrong he was. At the time I think I was numb; it was too much, all of those voices and opinions and stories of her. I let them wash over me.

Eirinie <eirinieeee@xmail.com >   Feb 17, 2016,
to Larissa   9:03 AM

My shmoo.
I had a dream i met you in another life
and I had to try and make you remember who
I was from the past one. It was a very sad
dream.

LA was good, just castings but work is
picking up in SF so that's good. Adam and
I are thinking of going on holiday for a
few days before he is back in the studio,
maybe New Orleans, maybe Mexico!
I'm training for a half marathon which is
13 miles and I am NOT ready....
What else? I miss you! How's Paris? Is it
cold? How are you and Pierre? What work
are you doing? Are you still in the same
apartment?

CHAPTER 27

DREAMS

I dreamt of you last night. Notable because it is so rare for me, although I wish for it constantly. Pierre told me about a year ago of a dream he had of you, so fleshed-out and real, such true closure, that it made me jealous. You visited him, took him to some magical, station-like place, you said goodbye to him, told him it would be the last time he saw you. I wanted to see you, ethereal and beautiful as ever, telling me you loved me, bidding me farewell. Why did he get that and I didn't?

Wait, that's not true. There was one. A few days before your funeral I dreamt you shook me awake, excitedly asked "Who is coming?" and I knew you meant "Who is coming to my funeral?" and I replied, flustered, "Everyone," and the answer pleased you as I thought it might and that was the end. An encounter so true to you that I was momentarily impressed with my brain's ability to so accurately re-create you for a tiny moment before wondering if, perhaps, somehow, that was really you?

But this dream. Last night's dream. I was in Paris, lost and wandering, unsure of where I would sleep that night, scenery ever changing as it so often does in dreams, and you came up to me. I asked if I could see your apartment, the one you died in. Not to go inside, just to stand outside looking up as you must have done so many times. You were grudging, didn't want to show it to me but it was all I wanted and so you obliged. We walked for a long time, I half recognised the route even though that didn't make sense, I had never been to that apartment, didn't even know which arrondissement it was in, but eventually we got there and you had a flatmate, another thing that wasn't true. She was blonde and lovely, a Claudia Schiffer type, doing her hair in the hallway mirror. She greeted you with that lazy familiarity shared by flatmates and you breezed by her. I was nervous, didn't really want to be inside, had told you I'd wanted to stand outside so why was I here? And then your face changed and even in the dream I knew it wasn't you, not really. You began tugging on my arm, telling me to come see what was in the bathroom and I knew you meant you, you were in the bathroom.

Claudia freaked, scared as if this had happened before and she knew what was in the bathroom and didn't want to see, and I freaked too. We locked ourselves in a cabinet that only closed two-thirds of the way and so there was just enough gap for your scrawny little wrists to jam through, grabbing mine, your face a twisted smile in the doorway, pulling me, insisting I come.

I woke afraid and rattled, that wasn't what I had wanted. To walk side by side with you through your beloved Paris, yes, but not to see. I couldn't see that. I don't think I can see that and simultaneously hold what was beautiful and timeless about you.

poo bear

Larissa <larry67@xmail.com>   Feb 28, 2012
to me

omg i cant believe you havnt sent me a
message in like actual DAYS
im so upset
where are you and why are you not here. do
not speak to me until it is
to ask about booking your ticket to
paris!!!!!!!!!!
you HAVE to come soon or i will never
forgive you
i am coming to london this weekend - the
show is this weekend and i
think mama thinks you are working for us
too?? xx

THE DEAD ARE GODS

I am not really a believer. The best way to describe myself would be atheist, but then again, I do like the idea of something greater than the universe, just not necessarily an old man with a beard keeping score. I have never been a fervent believer in anything, not in my little born-again Christian primary school in South East London, not in the Catholic all-girls school where mass was mandatory, not even in the Russian Orthodox church in which I was raised. And Orthodox churches are pretty mystical, a lot of smoke and low voices and all that dizziness because you have to stand throughout—a sort of out-of-body experience. Even that never swayed me into religion. In fact, the most diligent I have ever been with prayers and worship is with you, Larissa.

My mother is a talented iconographer. Some of my most nostalgic smells that take me back to my childhood are those of the tempera and the varnish, the smell of her solemnly finishing her painting, the praying that took place before she even started. I think I should like to paint you, Larissa. I think this is what I am doing as I write. This book begins with a prayer, a hope that my aim is true, that my writing is, in essence, a way of me completing the picture of you, varnishing it, waiting for it to be blessed.

In the Russian Orthodox church, icons are significant. Painting an icon takes time. It is a measured, almost formulaic process. There are some meditative qualities to it, a rhythm in their rote composition. First, you must know your saint. You must know their lives, know the aspects of them that are important to bring out. Were they a teacher? A student? Were they martyred? How did they die? They must be like a friend to you, a beloved family member. You ready the board; you sand and prepare your wood, cover it in gesso, a centuries-old primer. Not just any wood, it cannot be too hard, resinous woods leak sap over time, warping in different temperatures. Birchwood and cedar are good choices, limewood is cheaper, stable. The paint pigments can come in powder but some you have to grind, on a piece of glass using a large, flat glass grinder and water, or you can refine the paint with egg as if preparing a meal. For the egg concoction, the tempera, you only use the yolk, the pure protein with vinegar and water and it acts like a natural polymer. The thing with egg, my mother explained to me, is that the protein hardens with exposure to oxygen and so the paint becomes harder and harder over the years, meant to last generations of faith. Icons are painted to last a minimum of five hundred years and egg tempera, when properly done, will last well over that, as seen in the churches in Mount Athos and Mount Sinai, testaments to the process. Like the remnants of a fried egg left on a plate, dried.

Then comes applying the paint to the board, a process religious in its specificity. The darkest layer goes first, and then you would move to lighter paint, building up to even lighter layers, reflecting the movement from darkness to the lightness of revelation. It is important to remember that each brushstroke is a step toward knowledge, toward understanding, toward a closer relationship with your god. Next, the facial details, those long noses and broad nostrils so classic in Orthodox icons, a face that is facing you, unshrinking, unrepelled by your fallibility. A top layer of paint goes on, the lightest, the final stage, to symbolise the illumination of eternity shining out of the subject of the icon because the subject is now forever enshrined, you have made them infinite. You varnish with linseed oil, sealing it, before handing it to the church where a new icon typically sits on the altar for a week after being blessed.

During this whole process, it is customary to pray before you paint, but the best thing is to take part in the eucharistic life of the church, including attending services, going to confession, receiving communion, so that you yourself, the artist, are as close to your god and your saints as you can be, in order to better communicate that closeness onto the board. You are never far from God when you are creating an icon.

What is this book if not an icon to you? I have never been closer, never examined your life quite like this, who you are, what you wanted. There is an intimacy in my loss of you, I can get closer than you would have perhaps allowed me when you were living, I can examine things about you without being rebuffed, closing that inner door of yours on me. Now I feel as if I am in a museum, or

rather a church, in front of a painting (or rather, an icon), study-
ing you in this frozen tableau of life, finding myself closer to you
as I see your colours, the darkness moving to light, the two raised
fingers of your hand to symbolise a teacher. Because you were my
teacher in so many things, and even in death you move in myste-
rious ways, you teach me still. Writing this book has taught me
things about myself, my ability to understand, my capacity for
love, what it means to love beyond death.

You never frame an icon, my mother told me. You do not
frame it because the images are representing people who are still
here but invisible, and to put frames around them would be to create a break between our world and theirs. Fencing them in, limit-
ing them. Restricting our ability to connect. And so, death is not
the final door, slammed in my face. It is a gate, I can see over it
and beyond, I can find you still even though you are not living
anymore. I cannot touch you but I can see you, I can feel you, I can
hear you. And what else is love if not belief?

In the Orthodox faith, we kiss our icons. When we would
visit the cathedral in Ennismore Gardens—which took two
very long buses to get to from our South East London home to
Knightsbridge—we would often seek out our saints, the icons that
meant the most, and light a candle in front of them, kiss their edges.
I wondered about this, I wondered whether this was idolatry, I
wondered what it meant to kiss an inanimate object with such pi-
ous reverence, but my mother explained, "We kiss them because
they are people that we love, even if they are dead, and would
you ever come into a room and not kiss me, or Adam, or your

grandmother, or your daughter?" It was then that I understood the icons are an extension of the people we wish to feel with us once again, the people we love. I forgive myself this idolatry, Larissa. I allow myself to pore over our history, to kiss our corners, to light my candle every time I sit down at this keyboard.

The icon almost always squarely faces the viewer, which my mother says is important. The whole aim in life, she says, is to be seen as we are, by God, by others. A true representation of who we are, no hiding, an acceptance of the flaws with the good, and so the saints and the holy people in the icons face us, dead-on, and we face them. And we are accepted. I want to do this with you, too. I want to face you, I want to turn you and position you so that you can face me, and I want us to look at each other with acceptance. There are things I know about you now, Larissa, that are difficult to reconcile with who you were with me when you were alive. Somehow, I must find a way through the stories I tell myself about you, the facts at my disposal, and somehow, I must end this all by looking at you, straight-on, and understanding.

The saint in the icon is not only a witness but a reflection, too. Because in this journey to understand my loss, your death, our love, I have created a mirror in which I can see myself, and so to stand and look at you is also to stand and look at myself. But I suppose it was always like that, we were always similar, I just see it more clearly now.

This book is a hagiography. I have sainted you; I have anointed you and you have become more than my memories. You are made flesh. But in telling a saint's story you must be true, you must acknowledge the holy things, yes, but you must also acknowledge the ways in which they were fallible humans, because in the fallibility lies what makes them saints. For a long time, Larry, you were infallible to me, a deity, your physical beauty alone seemed unearthly. You seemed so much more than me, so above me, in intelligence and wit and presence. But I understand now that this is not how I best remember you, this is not how I best honour my love of you. Because to love you truly is to turn my body to face yours, to look at your truths, to look at the things you hid from me and from others who loved you, and say, I love you not in spite of but because of all that you were. Even the murky, even the things that I want to pack away into a box in the attic and pretend are not part of your history. I want to hold it all, the beauty and the blood, I want to redeem you and I want to be redeemed.

Sometimes I want to bring you back, like Lazarus. I want to resurrect you from your tomb. I have questions, I have answers, I have things I would like to do with you. But really, in writing this book I have realised that perhaps you are the resurrector, bringing me back from the living death of grief. In memorialising, I have found a way that the death of you can create life in me. What I am reluctant to do, what I am worrying I am doing is writing a towering testament. Descending from the mountain, stone tablets in hand—"This is who she was, this is her history." But what do any of us truly know about the interior lives of the people we love? I was stunned to learn things after you died, stunned that there was so much never told to me. I am trying to carve your story not in stone but in the sand, aware that when the tide comes it will be washed away, or changed some. I am aware that there are people who knew you who will read this book and will have their own version of events. I am trying to be as clear and as honest as I can in order to make a path for these other stories.

I spoke to your mum yesterday. She has not found a similar peace and I don't know how to fix that. I feel a little like a door-to-door preacher when I speak to her. I have my sermons, I can hold and pat her hand, try to make her listen, but she is somewhere else. Somewhere darker than I am, somewhere that is hard to reach. I don't think I can help her, not even with this book. It was my intention to bring some healing, some light, but perhaps I can only bring that to myself. Perhaps it is not for me to try to drag your mother to the place I find myself in. Perhaps all I can do is to show her the church I have built, show her the incense and the choir, invite her to stand with me.

My own mother told me just the other day, "We find it very difficult to believe we can be loved because of who we are, usually it is transactional, we are loved because we do the right things. It's very painful to love people when they're not being easy to love." But isn't that when we really love someone? Isn't that indicative of a love that is beyond the surface, beyond the day-to-day, a deeper love that probes, that ever-elusive unconditional love? Isn't the love I share with Adam this way, unflinching? We often say to each other, "There is nothing you could do that would repulse me." Because we know each other, we know the boundaries and borders that mark our personality, the things we find funny the things we find sad, we know each other so well that even a trespass, even a sin would be understood. I love him even when he is not being easy to love. I love you, Larissa, even though you were not always easy to love.

I love you in the face of many home truths, of many revelations, I love you even after you are long dead, it turns out. The lives of holy men and women are a crucial portion of the Bible. It is important, it contextualises and humanizes a whole faith. And so, Larry, does your life. It symbolises love, it symbolises friendship and sisterhood, it is so much more than the way in which you died. You are so much more than how you died.

The Russian Orthodox church always seemed transcendental, even if it didn't move me to faith. The services last hours and hours, are laden with heavy smoke from incense, the atmosphere is close and it is almost celestial. The choir that is often present lead the mood with slow, minor harmonies, and I can never shake the haunting memory of standing in line, waiting to receive communion, and hearing the traditional hymn ("Of the body of Christ take ye, of the well of immortality taste ye") sung up high behind me, lilting, dizzying. Visibility is low during the service, and only the people truly in need of a seat will sit. There are no pews, the few chairs available are scattered about the room, old babushkas taking a moment to sit, or the occasional pregnant woman. The presence of chairs would instill a hierarchy—in other types of churches there were specific pews for the donating patrons, the poor people, the undesirables. In the Orthodox faith one stands to pray because we are equal to God and equal to the saints we see on the walls. Standing imparts dignity. There is freedom in the worship, one can move around the church freely, with no boundaries.

I have seen grown men faint during services, from the heady aroma of the incense, from the standing. I learnt young how to stand for long periods of time—legs slightly parted, firm, I never needed the chair but definitely wanted one. It was an exercise for me, to see if I could, a competition with myself to distract from the glacial pace of the liturgy, which was often in Russian. An endurance test. I was good at it. People would compliment my mother on my behaviour, they would think I was enraptured with the church, mesmerized by the priest. And there was something mesmerizing about it all, for sure, but mostly I was just trying to withstand.

It has been a long time, maybe a decade since the last time I witnessed an Orthodox ceremony. I am not religious but I miss the ritual. I miss the quiet endurance; I miss the smell of myrrh and the sound of the chain of the censer clinking as the deacon sways it around the room. I miss the taste of Holy Communion, the prosphora chunks floating in wine in a gold chalice, I miss the ornate vestments of the clergy, often completed with a long, grey beard. I miss the pomp and circumstance of the liturgy, not dissimilar to the Catholic Mass, but with more heart. Perhaps this is why the way in which I worship you feels so familiar, so comforting—because I was trained from a young age to listen in silence, to withstand, to endure.

I say your name most days, I can often be found murmuring whispered prayers to you. Is this idolatry? I have your photo as the background on my phone, it is the first thing I look at in the morning and the last at night. It is like my saint card, and I clutch it close and try to read the answers in your eyes. My writing desk is now a small altar to you, a photo of you from a shoot, Paris in the background somehow still not as beautiful as you are. Were. Are? The pages of my book taped to the walls, I am a religious zealot in that room, I pace and mark the walls and rearrange your story, trying to find the truth, trying to tell the story of an angel.

I think you would be uncomfortable with this amount of worship. I think you might cringe, tell me to take stuff down. But perhaps you would also be moved, perhaps if you saw my dedication to you even after death you would know the depth of my love. You would know my reluctance to accept the presumed finality of loss. You would know that I seek to resurrect you with any means necessary. You would know I am devout.

I saw my first dead body in a church. An open casket, traditional in the Orthodox religion. The cathedral we frequented was dark, I am not sure I ever saw it with lights on, the sun pouring through the sporadic windows did little to illuminate anything but the hypnotic swirls of incense smoke, the choir above and behind me, a cacophony of voices as if from the heavens and, then, a corpse. In the Orthodox faith, the dead one is still a member of the congregation and I think I sensed this as a child, that the dead body was just another person. I don't recall being scared despite my youth. I remember there was something peaceful about it, something that didn't feel sad. An acceptance, perhaps. The lady had been old, no one was crying, it felt respectful and calm. The service continued and I assume later she was buried. It felt like just another part of the day.

When you died, when I went to your funeral, I felt disbelief. Sorrow. I wanted to see your body because I wanted to know it was true, because it didn't feel true, it felt like a cruel joke was being played on me, I needed to see your face. Like St. Thomas, I needed to put my finger in the marks of the nails. I needed to feel the pain of reality because I felt as if I was floating in a dreamlike sea, such was the dissonance between you being dead and the insistence I had in my gut that you weren't, couldn't be. Perhaps that is why I clutch your stories so close to me, because I must feel them, feel the viscosity, feel the weight of it all, some sort of self-flagellation to bring me closer to you, to prevent me from forgetting who you were, what you meant. It is my penance for not saving you, for not being a better friend, for not seeing the path you were on, not helping you get off it.

But once I finish writing, then what? How can I move on? I cannot just light a candle once a year on the twenty-fourth of September. I cannot just sever the ties I have to you, my ardent worship. I cannot let my remembering of you take the tone of a weary Christian going through the motions every Sunday, dutiful but absent. Surely the work I have done to remember you, to look at your life with an unflinching honesty and faithful kinship, surely that will mean you are eternal. Surely, in my grief, I have made you a god. I have made you the god you were always destined to be and now, because of my devotion, I will be rewarded with you for always.

I wonder if this is how Jesus's disciples felt. Because, when he died, it must have felt like it did when I laid my palm on top of your coffin—empty, final, quiet. The stark, cold reality of the proximity of your corpse a reminder that all of my magical thinking had been in my head. But then, three days later the disciples saw an empty tomb, the emptiness had the opposite effect, the emptiness was not a void but full of promise, a series of possibilities. And when I left Paris and was far from you and yet still the notion of you, the image of you was vibrant in my head, when I could still imagine exactly your reaction to whatever situation, the act of imagining felt like a possibility. The possibility of life after death, the possibility that you, and all that you were, did not vanish but remain here with me, immortalised in egg and paint and wood.

Larissa <larry67@xmail.com>   Jun 22, 2009
to me

my pookles i love you so muuch please dont
be sad again
your so beautiful and intelligent and
caring and your my best friend dont know
what id do without you, don wory we will
make the best plan ever, start afresh in
september but we have to plan it so we
can look forward to it!! well go somewhere
nice just me and you!

love you see you soon x x x x x x x x x x x

HEALING

My grandmother died almost fourteen years ago. I loved her so dearly and she was one of my favourite members of my family, if not the favourite. Quiet, calm, methodical, a gardener, a painter, a soother. It was my first loss, the first taste of loss and the most bitter. I think I wept for her for four years. When I told my therapist this recently, she said it sounded as though I didn't really heal well after it. This sounds blunt, as if to reinforce the idea that there's a designated time frame for mourning, but I think now I get what she meant.

I was inconsolable about my Nan for years. Truly could not bring her up without sobbing or just being brutally heartbroken over again. Now after two years of grieving Larissa, I can see the difference in the mourning. Yes, I am still occasionally devastated when I think of Larry, I will always feel bereft of her but something also feels healed. There is a contentment to where I am, perhaps. A coming to terms may be a better way of putting it. I bring her up at parties, in conversations, to my daughter, I talk of her casually, anecdotally, and when I do, I do not always feel that pull at the back of my throat that indicates I will soon be crying.

What is the difference? What is the difference between this Eirinie and the one of thirteen years ago, who felt as if a stone was tied around her waist as she floated in the ocean, desperately kicking her legs to keep from going under? More self-examination perhaps. Or just . . . more facing of the music. My Nanny dying was too painful to look at, I was too young to see how the loss was bleeding into the rest of my life, affecting my daily mood for years and years. With Larissa I felt as if I could do nothing but stare it down, and I was in a better place to do so. I had a husband who I knew would not let me sink, I had a daughter who forced me to put one foot in front of the other, which is all you can do in the throes of grief, I had nothing but pictures and emails and voice notes from her to stare at day after day, facing the absence of her instead of turning away.

I stared it down, all that pain. It is important to note that it didn't feel like I was doing anything courageous at the time, quite the opposite. I felt like I was sinking into the quicksand of despair and would never find my footing to get out, never relax enough to wiggle my shoulders free or whatever the fuck you're supposed to do in quicksand. But then, one day, who can say when but definitely within the past year, I found myself halfway there. Fingers moving, lungs expanding and contracting, eyes alert, almost out.

I don't say this to suggest there is a way to fully extract yourself from the pain of loss, that there is a day you can brush the sand off and never look back. Just because you climb out doesn't mean you won't find yourself there again, won't wake up one morning and feel that sticky weight on your limbs again, realise you won't see your person again, feel that hopeless despair. But at least when I find myself (often inexplicably) back in the quicksand there is a tiny part in my brain that knows I can get out. It has been done before so that means it can be done again. Maybe not right that second, maybe right that second I just need a cry or an angry walk or to talk to Maddy or Simon or another of our mutual friends. But one day, hopefully soon, I can find a way out again. The quagmire is ever constant and all around but once you get used to the new terrain, the panic of "Will I feel this way forever?" seems to be a little less urgent.

Perhaps that is the contentment I spoke of earlier. Not that I am now at peace with the fact that Larissa is dead, but instead that I am now at peace knowing I will never be at peace with the fact that she is dead. I won't forget her, I can't. Grief has a way of tugging at your sleeve and coughing politely. It'll be there if I think I've forgotten everything or not. And there is a little, perhaps slightly macabre, comfort there. My grief is no longer something I can ignore or block out or not look at, it can and will catapult me back to the boggy mess soon enough, and sure I'll get more dexterous at getting out but I'll still be there, feeling sad or bereft or lonely or broken. In a dark and yet not entirely depressing way, I sort of appreciate my new albatross.

As I headed into my twenties, I felt malleable. I was whatever anyone wanted me to be, I thought that's just what I'd do forever—mirror the people I was around when none of the people I was around were, frankly, worth mirroring. But Larissa. Larissa wouldn't stand reflections, that didn't interest her. She could see the inauthenticity of someone simply mirroring her and so in order to impress her I had to be me. I had to figure out who the fuck that was and luckily for me and maybe also her, she liked that person. And I slowly started to like that person too.

But I digress.

My malleability meant I couldn't dwell too long on grief over my grandmother, I didn't want to be the sad girl even though I undoubtedly was, and so I pushed my sorrow down. But now, in Larissa's absence, I have the capacity for self-reflection. It's okay for me to be sad in the life I've built for myself. I am practicing honesty with my child, showing her that sadness isn't taboo, it's as regular as happiness and just like happiness, it must be experienced. A gloomy mood does not make my husband turn from me, repulsed by my unsexiness. Instead, he turns toward me, a step or two away as he knows I do not like to be smothered, and he waits for me to tell him what I need.

Perhaps that is the fundamental difference between two deaths of two of the most important women in my life—growth. And I don't mean to say that to grow you must be married and have a kid, neither of those things are imperative to be an adult, but that somehow, finding my way through the brambles of my late teens into the wilderness of my early twenties I found a way to be truly, honestly myself and in doing so created a safe space for sadness, pain, shame, and disappointment. All those things we are told to hide. In embracing them I have found some sort of equanimity.

And so, thinking back to that lost little girl masquerading as an adult who lost her grandmother and couldn't find a way to sit with it, I see where I misstepped. Not by any fault on my part but just inexperience, ignorance. I didn't know that to look directly at my blinding sadness, at the bright sun of my loss was to take a little in. Just a little of the sadness in and it would help me, later, to fight off other rays of sadness or at least learn how to withstand their glare. I thought that to look at it I would immediately turn to stone and that would be it for me. A mental breakdown maybe, a suicide attempt. I didn't realise that by not allowing these feelings I was almost guaranteeing both things.

Maybe this all sounds very pessimistic, that you have to be sad to be okay. I don't know if that's the truth but I do know that, for me, accepting a bit of the darkness helped me see the light. I needed to get in it, really get wet or sandy or sunburnt or whatever metaphor worked for you, in order to find my footing. My path through one of the worst things I have ever experienced was simply that—to experience it.

Larissa <larry67@xmail.com>   Feb 24, 2016
to me

yep still with P id tell you if that wasnt
so poopoo!!!
yeh of course still see ████ too hes like
my only friend here
hes sweet he gave me some money the other
week when he just got bk from tour he was
like LOADED i read somwer that hes like a
millionair which i dont know if thats tru
but appaz from touring with ███ ████ he
got paid like millions well im not sure
about that but he definitely got bank
thats all i no
poopoo what will u do after modelng? i
mean its just odd jobs for me like bar
work and stuff do u thin u will do that
too or what? do u think about stuff?
yeh everyone in my building is decked out
in chanel and cant afford cheese right
now its a joke! lols
xxx

SINGER-SONGWRITER

When Larissa met the singer-songwriter who in many ways would, if not seal her fate, then send her down a path so unknown to the rest of her friends, I had been wary. She told me he was clean now, sober and married or maybe just had a girlfriend but some female indicator of stability, some sort of respectability. I was dubious, I didn't know him personally but I knew of him, I'm not sure there's a British person alive who was semi-conscious during 2003–2009 who didn't, and I knew the things he was associated with. I didn't love this for Larissa but I also knew just how many of our peripheral friends did hard drugs, people we saw at parties or on shoots, not close enough friends to be a threat but close enough to see, to know. My father has had substance abuse issues since I was a child and so whenever the topic came around, I would close up, shut down. I didn't want to hear about it, I didn't want to know the things that made that drug so desirable to someone I mourned as if he really were dead, not just living in Catford.

So, when Larissa brought the singer up, I blanched, made some vague blanket threat about her being careful around him but when I look back and reexamine that moment, I do not recall feeling fear that she would do those things, that she would touch a needle. For me that was a line never to be crossed, taboo but easy to avoid. It didn't attract me in the least and I suppose my mistake was assuming that she felt the same way.

The singer helped her with her literary magazine, he made it popular in a way that she was certain would have been impossible without him. People bought it at his shows, he was synonymous with poetry and that whole beatnik vibe, in no small part because of his habit. The one time I almost met him was Larissa's birthday when I had travelled to Paris just for her. She and Pierre had fallen out, a huge row that ended with something being thrown by someone, I forget, and so instead of merely meeting me at the Eurostar and going to dinner, she had shown up with a suitcase and it was clear she would be staying with me. I was secretly thrilled, as I was not looking forward to navigating Paris by myself with only my GCSE French skills to get me by. Larissa was fluent in that effortless way that made native-born Parisians presume she was French. Being in Paris with her was like being led by the hand through the most beautiful city, whispering your desires and having them be translated and then manifested before your eyes. She was magical and I was mute. A gift.

She met me, we dressed up for her birthday. To the nines, as was expected. Occasions, for her, were celebrated with gusto, with your full chest, with no fucking care in the world about how out of place you might look dressed in a white satin jumpsuit and baby-blue suede shoes in a dive bar. The plan on her birthday was to go to a fancy hotel bar, drink twenty-euro cocktails, and meet the singer afterwards, maybe at a house party or one of the cooler bars near his apartment. But the singer was unavailable. We had to assume this as he didn't respond to her texts, didn't pick up the phone. Larissa seemed unbothered, whereas I wondered to myself why the fuck one of her closest Paris friends would choose to be MIA on her birthday. Now, from all this distance I can see that the reason the singer did not respond was and always would be drugs. So many clues slipping into place far too late for me to do anything useful with them.

Was she doing drugs that night? I don't know. Did she do them when she got back to the apartment, when I stayed with Natalia at the club, dancing 'til two, and then walked across the city with her, heels in hand, one of my favourite Paris experiences? I don't know. I know that I got back and Larissa was asleep with her iPad on, playing one of her awful shows. I crawled in beside her and we slept, emerging only when we were too hungry to stay in bed.

That was a funny trip. Funny as in odd. It was so lovely to have her to myself. I had anticipated sharing her with Pierre, perhaps having to go off on my own adventures as she conducted her regular life, but instead we slipped back into our old patterns, sleeping late, ordering food, getting dressed up, going out. Sitting in our comfortable silence, a puddle that has since become an ocean. I am used to not hearing her, I realise now. I am used to it because often we wouldn't talk for a whole day despite being right next to each other.

There was a real wonder in that, I have yet to make a friend with whom I can do that, where the quiet means nothing, is not weighted with emotion or expectation but is simply silence. A purity in that kind of comfort, a letting down of guards. And so, if I am so used to not hearing her perhaps that explains why now, so many, many months since her death, I am unfazed by her absence. Or, rather, unflustered. Comforted by the silence. There is something nice in that symmetry, a continuation of her life in her death. Perhaps with her silences, with our mutely agreed upon days of quiet, she was preparing me for today, when the quiet would become a given.

But that trip was odd because, despite slipping on that noiselessness, the atmosphere was different. I wonder if I am reimagining things with the knowledge I possess now. I wonder if it truly was so, because in my memory there was something else in the room with us. Something else I couldn't get her to say. I pressed for details about Pierre, what she would do, what did she need, was there somewhere else for her to stay when I left Paris in a few days? But she gave me sparse details and then said she didn't want to talk about it, which with Larissa truly meant she didn't want to fucking talk about it, don't bring it up again. That something else took up a lot of space in the room, it puzzled me and I was on edge, I remember when I finally got back on the Eurostar to head back to London I was relieved, I felt like a pressure valve had been turned and my nerves settled.

Saying that now, it seems fairly clear that most definitely in my subconscious if not in my conscious mind I was aware that something was not right. In my logical mind I know that it is with the benefit of hindsight that I feel that way, that there is no way I knew back then what I know now. But in my illogical, emotional mind I think, often, why didn't I do more? What was I thinking? My friend was going through something that I couldn't access and instead of pushing, instead of digging, I allowed her to take the lead and decide what we would address. And so now, fucking now, two and some years after Larissa dies, here I am like an unfunded archaeologist, digging for bones, unearthing whole skeletons of huge beasts that once roamed my world, finally saying, "Oh, that's what they are." But it's too fucking late. Because what now, Eirinie? What now? I resurrect these bones, allow them to live again? No. I painstakingly reassemble them, I parade them around, I prop them in a museum and charge for admission to this dead landscape that helps no one.

Who am I helping with this writing? Not Larissa, for she is dead and as much digging as I am doing I will not change what happened to her, I will never uncover anything she didn't leave out for me to find, certain things will remain deep under the earth. Is it for me, this self-flagellating, this reminiscing? Building a monument to someone who will never see, the one person I would like to see?

There is some catharsis for sure, there is some reburying. Perhaps that is actually what I am doing, unearthing the truth to understand a person who could not, would not be fully understood in life. There are aspects to this book that flesh out who Larissa was in a way that could not have been accessed without me digging, without the reanimation. In a way I am continuing our friendship, because a friendship should be one in which you continually grow and evolve and, little by little, discover things about the other person, maybe a little about yourself too. Perhaps this book is a discovery.

more ranting

....

 Larissa <larry67@xmail.com>   Jun 3, 2009
to me

ok i am officialy leading a useless life
i have watched 3 films onling today,eaten
more than i care to remember and smoked
about 40 fags o and finished off a bottle
of red
to make things worse the last film i
watched was confessions of a shopoholic

when you get back we need to make our
lives meaningful

this summer we are gonna rip it up

that means using ALL of our sponsers for
good purposes (of course this means lunch
and dinner ;)
i so wish we could afford an apartement :(

ok love you
cant wait to see you when you get back

so somerset next weekend???

....

FULL DISCLOSURE

I f you have ever lived in London, if you have ever been young in my city, if you have ever been a part of a group of friends who liked to go out, you have probably done cocaine.

I have done cocaine. It was casual and plentiful in the clubs and bars we went to, in the places I worked. It was more notable to have a friend who didn't do coke than one who did. This sounds excessive now, even to me and it was my lived experience. It sounds excessive because now my idea of a crazy night is a bottle of wine and the back catalog of *Cybill*, because I owe my children a life that does not include a waster of a mother. But back then, in my early twenties, it was casual. It was normal. In the modelling world it was like smoking, no big deal. Yeah probably not great for your health but we were young and stupid and arrogant and convinced we would be fine. And we were. All of the people I have ever done coke with are now legitimate adults with homes and mortgages and children and careers and functioning lives. It didn't impede our ability to find some semblance of normality, it didn't turn into a gateway drug.

I bring this up because, in discussing Larissa's life and her death, I want to be clear on my part in things. I did not introduce Larry to coke but I had done it with her multiple times. In hindsight, in light of what happened to her, I feel disgusting saying this, as if it were me who pushed her down the path she ended on, but to say that is to deny her own volition. I do not wish to absolve myself nor do I think I deserve blame. I want to be honest. I want to be clear. I want to acknowledge that we, Larissa and I and all of our friends, were part of a scene that made certain types of drug use commonplace. Weed and coke were commonplace. I have never seen anyone shoot up in real life, I have never been in the same, tight crew as someone using heroin (to my knowledge). How did I not see the link? Why did I think that just because I had escaped the London party circuit unscathed, because I had found a way to drink less and not do blow, it meant that Larissa would also slip out the same way? I should have realised when she made friends with the singer-songwriter that the Venn diagram of people we both knew and hung out with was being severed, that she was moving into a different circle, one I had no foothold in, one I had no knowledge of. I wasn't paying attention. That is hard to say but it is true. Not that I think I could have prevented what happened to her but by god I could have borne witness, I could have cautioned, I could have watched.

I vacillate with this feeling—that I could have been a better friend, that I could have stood beside her more conscientiously—and then the deep-in-my-soul knowledge that I know who Larissa was, I know what she would have allowed me to see, I know that she was a particular person who did things her own way. I know that both of these things will continue to circle my head like a cartoon character, concussed with tiny birds floating around their head, dazed.

Larissa <larry67@xmail.com>   May 31, 2012,
to me   3:29 AM

poo bear
i will be in london next week. i arrive
on tue. my mum and luth will be in ghana
so i will be lonely!!! you have to keep me
company!!!
when does a get to london?
how are you?
an th ebloody hell are you gonna install
skype woman! xxxxxxxxxx

LONDON

London is almost too hard for me now. Too many memories, too many places I can imagine you walking into; too many places I have stood smiling at you. As I sit in the PizzaExpress Jazz listening to a band I know you would not like with a bottle of merlot (your favourite) across from me as if to remind me that this is what you'd be three glasses into by now. Even more painful that I can imagine exactly how you'd behave—you'd show up, late, and move a chair so your body would touch mine and give me four or five quick kisses on my cheek whilst I shooshed you, then you'd take a sip of my wine, listen to the music for a few minutes before getting up to order your own. We'd leave early to go somewhere quieter, or fancier depending on who's paying. I'd get us a taxi home and it would make you so happy. You loved taxis home. Taxis anywhere to be honest.

I was so good at making you happy, I knew all the triggers. Cabs home at the end of the night (fun or disastrous, it didn't matter), takeout when you were hungry and all we had was an egg and a half-eaten jar of peanut butter, surprise presents of any sort. Your love language would have been tokens of affection, if I had ever managed to get you to do that quiz. The other things I provided, those unspoken, intangible things I knew also made you happy, but you also knew they would always be there. I made my reliability known constantly, to my detriment at times. This is my comfort and my eternal heart-stopping shame; you knew I loved you, but I also had not spoken to you in a few weeks at the end of your life, annoyed at you for something or the other. I think because you hadn't wished me happy birthday, but then I hadn't either and yours was two weeks prior to mine. You would have seen the WhatsApp messages read, but not known why I hadn't replied. Did you think about this at the end? Did you wonder where I was? If I knew? Did you have time to think about me? About anything?

I've been steadily skirting around this. The act of your death. Mostly because no one but you knows what happened—you were alone, for better or worse. You were found in the bath a week after you died, by Pierre and Simon and your landlord, who is faceless to me but who I am sure has never forgotten yours after that morning. The water was murky, the boys thought you had killed yourself at first but I knew you wouldn't have done that, not without reaching out to someone. You had done that before, a year or so ago, and I had picked up the phone and, although the line was muffled, I listened to you cry and evade my questions until I realised that all you needed was my ear and to hear my own muffled voice, saying "I'm here, I'm here."

This time there was no phone call. No crying. There was only a week in between my birthday and when I was told you were missing, when I had an unshakable gloom I could not explain to my husband, or anyone. I blamed it on the birthday but if time is a circle, perhaps, somewhere, I knew this moment. Knew it to be the last one I would have where we would share this planet alive together. The call came first from Maddy, who told me you were missing (before I walked into the ArcLight to see *Beautiful Boy*, a movie one should absolutely not see while your friend's whereabouts are unknown). I immediately panicked and also immediately sedated my panic, knowing how furious you would be to hear, later when you were found safe, that a global alert had been raised. I remember sending you a message, drafting it twice before settling for something with an air of nonchalance: "Oi. Where are you"; 3:09 p.m., the fourteenth, of October 2018. On the morning of the fifteenth, after struggling throughout the night with a child who would not sleep, my husband took our baby out of the bed so I could try to recuperate. Almost the moment they left the room, Natalia called me.

It's funny, I can reconstruct from the WhatsApp messages that I learnt you were dead just twenty-four hours after I was told you were missing, and yet I remember it lasting days, even weeks. Why is that? Did my worry and sense of foreboding stretch the time out over the loom of grief? So that, in my head, there was more of a chance for you? More of a chance for me to find you, perhaps on the next circle of time when I loop back through this moment? More of a chance to grab you before you slip through the cracks of this world?

Natalia was crying. She said my name, "Rinie," and I just knew. And I knew that I had known already, I had known for some time. And the impossibility and glaring reality of it made me moan out in that solitary bedroom lit by the rising sun so that my husband ran in. I do not remember what else Natalia said, I remember we sobbed together, I remember hanging up, I remember my husband's body near mine as I wailed, unable to voice the syllables needed to convey the message, but he knew. He staggered, or I remember him staggering. Our daughter came in the room, he did not know whether to take her away from me or stay and comfort me, and so we all wailed in that room together, all for different reasons.

Flicking through our WhatsApp chat, a fledgling thing of maybe a year or two, I find myself getting furious with past Eirinie for not responding to a question, or not booking a flight when you told me you were having a hard time after that breakup. That is the nature of those transatlantic chats—one person is paying attention but the other is off living life In a different time zone, and then it flips. I know that. I know there were times I needed you but you didn't reply. I know that. But I am still angry with myself, I wish I had given you every minute of my day, paid attention to every silly reference you made, why didn't I watch *The Adventures of Pete and Pete* and report back when you asked if I'd seen it as a kid and I told you we didn't have cable? Why didn't I listen to the Gun Club like you suggested? Why didn't I book a flight to Paris and take a week off to see you?

Maybe it wouldn't have mattered. Your mum was in Paris to visit and you didn't answer the door, that's how the alarm got sounded. We knew it was odd, as whatever your state you would force yourself to make time for her. You would hide your cigarettes, get rid of the empty wine bottles. But this time your mum stood on one side of your apartment door and knocked, called you, called Natalia, and the whole time you were on the other side, not moving.

Oh, my heart.

Poo poo

Eirinie <eirinieeee@xmail.com>   Dec 16, 2017
to larissa, Larissa, Larissa

My love!

My messages aren't going through on
whatsapp. Lemme know you're ok.

X

A VICTIMLESS CRIME

O nce again, I circumnavigate your death. Let's get to
the pith of this thing, that painful, bitter pith. You
were alone in the bath, maybe sleeping pills, definitely
a gin and tonic (the thought of which comforts me still). But wait,
not sleeping pills. Not more censorship. How do I get closer to
the truth of it all if I cannot acknowledge the few crumbs I have
at my disposal?

Chantal told me, even before you died, that she was worried.
Never did she say the word "heroin" but it was implied; she de-
scribed your sleepiness, inattentiveness, your inability to focus.
She was worried for you, I was too, but even then I couldn't see.
That was a crumb.

When you would ask me for money, paltry sums really but
sums I was reluctant to part with, something about your requests
bothered me and I could never work out, never spent time working out why. That was a crumb.

On that meandering stroll through French neighbourhoods with Pierre after your funeral, he told me that you would shoot up heroin between your fingers, your beautiful fingers or toes, so that no one would see the track marks. That was a fucking loaf.

And so, you died in the bath, after months of recovery and then a sudden relapse, of a heroin overdose. Too much. It is too much for me to take.

How long had it been going on? How long had it been right under our noses? What is it about addiction that makes people squirm, unable to look at the truth and say, I see you, I know you're trying, please let me help you? I wish I'd known; I wish I'd seen. What use am I now, figuring this out for you posthumously? How could I have made you feel less alone? I know this feeling of blame, I have felt this with my father, felt I could have done better and tried harder and made him stay, made him sober. But I know, rationally, that it was not my choice to make, not my history to change, and so it goes with you, too.

Did Pierre tell me before about the drugs? Did I know and forget? Did I hear and reconstruct the truth?

There is so much that I have reconstructed since your death. Your mum called me the other day with a specific question—did I know about the heroin? I said no, because it is the truth that consciously I did not, but I also told her that maybe somewhere in my head there was a part of me that knew and couldn't look at it. I told her about my dad, about his history with drugs and how I had

told you about him once, a long time ago, and I had so adamantly
denounced and vilified people with heroin addiction that I now
feared that was the reason you didn't tell me.

Was it?

Was that why? I know now that you had been clean, had been
working on being clean and finding the stability to keep your
streak going. Looking back at our constant back-and-forth I see a
watershed moment where you started asking about my child, about
me. We engaged in a way that was reciprocal and now I know that
you were doing better then. And I know when you relapsed too,
but only in hindsight. You became gloomier, you bemoaned life,
you seemed . . . sad. I didn't examine it too much then because we
both were subject to rapid mood changes. I thought you'd come
out of it, I'd see you at Christmas in London, you'd be better, I'd
be more focused on you, we'd drink and part knowing we'd see
each other again.

I keep playing back the trip to Paris. Natalia swears she told
me about the drugs but I can't recollect. Did my mind really do
mental gymnastics just to keep me "safe," to keep me from seeing
the truth? Do I know? Did I know? There are so many bread-
crumbs now, I'm like Hansel and Gretel tracing my way back to
the origin, white pebbles in the moonlight. I chastise myself for
not seeing them when I could have maybe done something. I am
not naive, I know I couldn't have fixed the addiction, I know that
those movie montages of someone barricading a friend going cold

turkey into their room whilst they vomit and shake and halluci-
nate but inevitably come out on the other side of it are not at all
realistic. My father was an addict, I know the difficulty of kicking
a habit like that. I know that you can't do it for anyone, not even
your children, desperate as they are for you to do so. But maybe, I
think, maybe I could have been your rock. I could have listened
and suggested and helped and counselled you back to life. Maybe
if I'd known, there would have been something for me to do. Now
I feel idle, I feel useless. What the fuck can I do now? I don't know
what to do with my hands. Writing is all I can do.

When I first heard you had died, all I knew was that it was in
the bathtub. My mind ran riot from there—suicide, sliced wrists,
overdose, murder even. I knew you were in that tub for a week,
I knew that Pierre and Simon found you, I wanted to know and
didn't want to know what you looked like. Simon said you looked
nothing like you.

Then someone, I forget who, said "pills." And "accidental."
And I clung to that because dear god thank god that is a narrative
I can get behind that this is a tragic mishap I can perhaps one day
utter out loud. It's sad but beautiful, terminal but clean. I can tell
that to the overly nosy people whose first question when I say my
friend died is "How?" I know that because she was young and cool
and vital it seems improbable that she would die and so people
inquire because they so desperately need to know that it won't happen to them. But that is such an insensitive question. It's painful to
answer, even when you do have a sterile go-to to throw out.

I am not certain how long I hung on to that excuse. Thinking back, I believe I knew that it wasn't the complete story, I just didn't have the details to fill it in and I wasn't sure I wanted them. The little that I knew almost destroyed me and I didn't know how I would hold the dear departed memories of you beside the gritty reality of your death. Strange bedfellows. And so, I held the truth tight like a shield to protect me but also to protect you because I have longed to protect you since the day I first met you. You were strong and powerful and vibrant, yes, but you also had a vulnerability, a naivete that expressed itself in your inability to grasp geography, your occasional ignorance of sex. (I remember once we were in Manchester with our friend Morgan, he made a joke about muff diving and you were baffled. What was it? We explained and you died laughing. You made elaborate diving motions between cackles, saying "Oh because you dive in! You dive in!!!")

Speaking to friends recently, I understand that the days and months after your death were peppered with clues, just like the days and months and years before, if I'm honest. The French police asking who gave you the drugs: I filed away as "pills, maybe oxy." Most tellingly the talk with Pierre about how you used to use: I filed it as "past tense." I didn't connect what he was saying with your moods and your absence. I suppose I have a little of your naivete, too. Because now I see what they were all trying to tell me. But I didn't hear it until Natalia, one day in a voice note on WhatsApp, said it plainly—heroin. I was taken aback, I stuttered in my reply to her. Asked her how she knew, who told her. This must have been a year, maybe a bit less, after you died. My denial and twisted self-preservation had withstood longer than I ever thought it could. Natalia seemed confused that I didn't know, and then she sounded guilty like she had broken the news to me although I now see that "the news" had been trickling into my ears from the beginning. Or was it the end?

I was reeling again just as I had when I first heard you were dead. I thought I was on sturdy footing and now here I was, poring over the case files in my head, connecting the past stories, the whispers from friends from years ago, the suspicious emails you sent, all these fucking clues so many fucking clues and I never solved the case. I had to be told the ending! What kind of a friend, what kind of a sleuth am I? It was the most paint-by-numbers mystery. I had the name of the villain in my hands before you fucking died alone in that bathtub. Why didn't I fix it? Why didn't I know why didn't I solve it? I felt like the detective in the show who has been rushing across town, always a beat behind the culprit, only to arrive at the final scene too late, too late. The girl is dead, the trail is cold, the killer is long gone.

The details suddenly become incredibly interesting to me. I know very little about the logistics and reality of heroin use, the actual experience of it. I know what the movies told me, I know it is meant to be the most indescribable joy the first time, I know I will never, ever get close to trying it because I can never reconcile the crimes my father committed against his family with whatever pleasure he may have gotten from it. I want to know more, but I also don't. It is like my overwhelming urge to google "body one week in bathtub," I want to know those last moments for you and the lingering, stagnant week that followed but I cannot. I cannot see that or know that. I saw what it did to Simon, seeing you like that. I know it will kill me.

I become very interested in news articles about drugs, I read the details about eyes rolling back, about the bruises in the crook of the arms from so many needles, about all the desperation. There is an opioid crisis, the papers declare. It is not news that is hard to find. I think about my dad in his midtwenties in the midnineties addicted to a drug that made him have no care for his obligations to his two small children, his worried wife. They told my mother, back when she tried to find him help, that he didn't qualify for rehab because he already had a support system in her. Wasn't that a crisis? Is it only a crisis when white people start to die?

There is a type of victim that is proven to get more traction in the news and with public sympathy than others. They are white, preferably blonde. Good family, nice smile. Led astray by something beyond their control, ruined by something not of their making. Murdered perhaps, mutilated and left for dead, stolen from their kids in the night. Even little lost children are only found when they are sweet white cherubs with dimples, a mourning picture-perfect family, a house with a garage. A drug addict is not sympathetic. We all know it is their fault, they chose to do that to themselves, they stole from their parents, they sold themselves for a fix, they left their babies with strangers so they could desecrate their own bodies.

I know how they are seen because I see my father like that. I have no sympathy; I feel nothing for his "situation." I think of how it affected me and my brother and my mum and I see the wreckage and I think, fuck him. But now it is different. Now it is you, a person I can say with confidence I knew better than my own father. My brain struggles to follow that same pattern of incrimination it did with my dad. I can't do that with you and so I have to look at it from another angle.

I know that if I mention the heroin to people, they will have a knee-jerk reaction. Somewhere in their minds against their better judgement they would dismiss you, relegate you to a pile of humans believed to be undeserving of grief and sympathy. A shrug, what-you-gonna-do, that's what she gets. Maybe in denying the truth over and over, covering my ears to the cockerel crowing, I was preserving your modesty, pulling the curtain to hide your nakedness. It wasn't honest but it felt right.

But how can we all be taught the humanity behind substance abuse? How can we see the fucking person and not the statistic? How can we move past our blame and our I-told-you-so's to find a place of empathy and understanding? I believe, by showing our loved ones. Here they are, they'd be pissed if they knew I was airing their laundry in public but by god you should know them. They were cherished and cared for and worried over and beloved and they are gone and don't need to be. You didn't need to be alone in a bathtub the way you were, tucked away out of sight for so long. You relapsed and felt too ashamed to tell anyone but your therapist about it, you most likely fell victim to the most common of drug deaths—you had been clean so long your body was no longer accustomed to the amount you would do, and so you did too much.

And you died.

This is the truth.

This is how you died.

I cannot be your true, unflinching friend if I do not look this in the eye, if I do not hold your ghost-hand and acknowledge it and love you despite it. It makes me think of the time we asked you to do a reading at our wedding and the other day I found the Nabokov excerpt from *Invitation to a Beheading* I had printed out for you amongst our wedding souvenirs:

> In spite of everything I loved you, and will go on
> loving you—on my knees, with my shoulders drawn
> back, showing my heels to the headsman and strain-
> ing my goose neck—even then. And afterwards—
> perhaps most of all afterwards—I shall love you, and
> one day we shall have a real, all-embracing explana-
> tion, and then perhaps we shall somehow fit together,
> you and I, and turn ourselves in such a way that we
> form one pattern, and solve the puzzle: draw a line
> from point A to point B . . . without looking, or,
> without lifting the pencil . . . or in some other way . . .
> we shall connect the points, draw the line, and you
> and I shall form that unique design for which I yearn.

HAPPY BIRTHDAYYYYYYY

 Larissa <larry67@xmail.com>   Oct 2, 2016
to me

HAPPY BIRTHDAY MY BEAUTY!!!!
whats the plan for today? I really hope u
have a great day
Miss you loads
let me know what u do to celebrate
all my love
HAPPY BIRTHDAY AGAIN XXXXX

THE BIRTHDAY PARTY

It was your birthday yesterday. I was rocked by queasiness, part the baby I am carrying, part the feeling I have nothing planned to celebrate. It feels like pressure. I woke up early several times last week in a panic that I had forgotten, that I had missed it. Hadn't done the obligatory Instagram post, had not raised a glass, hadn't even thought about you. But each time it was just a false alarm. I still had the time.

And yet when your birthday comes around, I have planned nothing. I feel immobile with the pressure. I should have something by now, surely? I bet Joan Didion does something elegant to commemorate her husband and daughter, I'm sure she has their favourite lunch at a restaurant with white tablecloths, takes a walk on their favourite hike, orders their favourite bottle of red. I know so much about what you liked, about the things that were your favourites, but I still feel paralyzed. Should I get a fancy bottle of merlot? Should I be ordering pizza and watching TV all day?

Should I be getting dolled up and going out into the world, a vintage dress, a red lip?

Instead, on your birthday, I do nothing. Next to nothing. I have a Zoom call with our mutual friends but it doesn't hit the spot like I was hoping, afterwards I feel drained and incomplete and I take a deep, unsatisfying nap. I have a glass of rosé, watered down with Pellegrino, and I smile for the first time thinking how you'd love pregnant me sipping on booze for you, a little devil-may-care, a little caution to the wind. You loved when I flirted with danger, it was so rare for me that you cheered me on, clapped me on the back. I often worried about things too much.

But what should I be doing? Perhaps I should take this time to have a plan in place? Perhaps if I thought about what you would do for me, if it were the other way around. I think you'd get drunk; I think you'd talk about me, I think you'd get dolled up.

I feel frozen by my lack of response. Incapacitated by choice.

How should I remember you?

Am I doing it right?

Is this enough?

Oi!!!

....

 Eirinie <eirinieeee@xmail.com>   Mar 22, 2015
to larissa, Larissa, Larissa

Shmooms.

Talk to me. What's going on? Are you ok?
I'm worried about you and we never talk
anymore and I don't like the thought of
you being sad so TALK TO ME

....

 Larissa <larry67@xmail.com>   Feb 10, 2016
to me

Fuck just got this!

....

HEROIN

I spent a lot of time fretting over what your final moments were, if there was a second of panic in your eyes, if you figured out what you'd done before it was through, or if you were oblivious. Did you start dying before you slipped in the water? I assume so, the cause of death wasn't drowning so you must have been dead before you slumped down. I wonder if you would have done anything different had I been able to, like the Ghost of Christmas Future, enter the room, tell you what was going to happen.

It's still so surreal to have you gone. It's still so odd to think about your vitality, particularly in my own life, and think of its absence. To think of what I took for granted when you were living, that I'd have time to see what was going on with you, that I'd have time to interrogate you and implement some change in your life. Time. I thought there was time.

Instead, here I am, typing into a timeless void, speaking my words for you into the universe and hoping against hope that you can hear and understand that I thought there would be time. It wasn't that I was neglecting you, Larry. I just thought there would be time.

Time became a fragmented concept for me the day you died. Of course, certain things kept on ticking, certain things like my child growing, like the deadline of us buying a house, these things served as handlebars for me on days when I wasn't sure what had happened or when, I could grab on and keep some semblance of forward momentum. But other things became hazy, I forgot the date of your birthday (was it the twenty-second or the twenty-fourth of September? Or was that my dad's?), I forgot how long it had been. Some days it didn't matter how far away I got from the horror of your final day; it could feel like today again. It could feel like it was happening right now and I was here, in California, six thousand miles away and incapable of stopping the inevitable. Sometimes I would wake in the night and my heart would lurch at the realisation you were dead, even though it had been two years.

Some days I would think of you and feel nothing. A shrug maybe, a "Well, it happened and there's nothing I can do about it." My heart felt stony on those days, impervious. Healed? No. But hardened. The pain felt less urgent, maybe.

To be honest I am not sure how many times I can write this. I don't feel like I am getting anywhere with your story, I feel like I am flogging a dead horse. I want closure, I want justice, I want answers but instead here I am, walking this dusty path back and forth so long I have made a divot and cannot get out. I am a Grecian cautionary tale come to life. There are no answers in your death, there are no answers in your life. What happened, happened, just like how the sky is blue today, just like how the buds in my garden will bloom, just like how my child will continue to sprout up into the world. These things just happen and in searching for answers I fear I will only find my own madness waiting for me. But how do I stop? How do I pump the brakes, decide I have had enough? How do I get you out of my head? I don't want you out of my head but I am not sure I can ever stop analyzing your life if you're not.

I feel trapped in a loop. It's Groundhog Day again. I can't get out.

Larissa <larry67@xmail.com>   Mar 27, 2012
to me

poops will u just book for wen ur bro
leaves town? need you soon or i might die!
wend to some bar for cocktAails yesta and
nearly had a heart attck
from all the hot guys i saw - I have never
actually looked at people
and though omg i want to have sex with
you!!! but wow! we r goin ther
for sure!
so girl time is much needed soon!!!

ADDICT

s heroin like bulimia or anorexia where you are never re-covered, always actively in recovery? I assume so. My dad was absent from my childhood, my brother's childhood, in a way that hurt us deeply and probably still affects us in some way to this day. I thought I'd never see him again, it was his death, not Larissa's, I spent my young life awaiting news of, certain that one day he'd fuck up and do too much or the wrong shit and just die. I thought about this so long that I was sort of numb to it. Just an eventuality of life, I thought. I think most that have loved people who struggle with substance abuse have steeled themselves to that possible eventuality.

My dad, Devon, stumbled back into my life on my wedding day of all days. I had invited him to the wedding because I thought that's what I should do. I knew he was trying to be sober, it seemed like the olive branch that an adult offers, proof that I wasn't the hurt child anymore but a mature person capable of burying the hatchet and moving on. It felt like a flick of my hair, sending that invite. I felt grown.

On the morning of my wedding he texted me, or called me, or maybe he spoke to my brother? He wouldn't be coming. Yes, that was it. My brother and my mum knew me well enough not to tell me. He said he couldn't find anything to wear, his suit he had planned on was still at the tailor's. My brother sobbed uncontrollably throughout the ceremony, which everyone thought was a testament to his love for me, and in part it was, but it was also because our father had been standing us up our entire lives. Our father, for whom we had waited at the window, watching for him until our mother peeled us away, had once again disappointed us at the most crucial time. I remember looking for him in the church. How could we forgive him now?

Unbeknownst to us, my dear friend and bridesmaid Rosie had quietly intervened, had her boyfriend in London meet my father at the train station, buy his exorbitant ticket (fuck you, South West Trains), calm the nerves he was vocal about, and send him down. Another family friend met him at the train station, brought a suit from a tall relative (Devon is six-foot-four), and brought him, late, to the reception. It was perhaps the kindest, most thoughtful gift I've ever received, and one I wasn't sure I even wanted.

Truth be told my heart sank a little when I saw him. I didn't want to play pretend, not on my wedding day. I didn't want to have to swallow my feelings and be the bigger person, play parent to my own fucking parent. But on his face I saw his fear, his apprehension and in an instant I realised how difficult it must have been for him to walk back into the lives of a family he left behind years ago, not just me and my mum and my brother but my grandfather who had bought his first passport so he could leave Jamaica and be with little baby-me, my uncles who loved him, family friends who vouched for him again and again. And so, I allowed it. I smiled, I hugged him, he told me I looked beautiful, he shook Adam's hand with all of the fatherly power he had left to wield. And as people got drunk, he blended in, he smoked weed with my brother, he danced somewhat inappropriately with my mother. He is in the pictures of my wedding, cemented in the only milestone of mine he managed to catch.

And then, four years later, when my first baby was not even a year old, he had a series of aneurysms. My brother had been visiting him, I had kept a loose (but substantial relative to our communication before) text conversation with him about his new fiancée and their child. It wasn't quite the father-daughter relationship I had hoped to forge if he ever got sober, but I took the crumbs because to a starved person they seemed like loaves.

The aneurysms began as headaches, he complained about one to my brother when they met up. They blossomed into a pain he had to be hospitalized for and the doctors told him (or my mother perhaps, who came down with the swiftness reserved for loved ones) that the decades of heroin use had left his brain more susceptible to damage than a man of his age would normally face.

They thought he would die. My mother called to warn me.

I had been preparing for that phone call my whole life. I didn't expect the circumstances to be as they were but I was supposed to be ready and I absolutely was not. The fear and the hurt and the anguish I felt were less about losing him, as I had already done that countless times, and more about the fear of never being able to say the things I wanted to say to him. I felt guilty for that selfishness. My sadness wasn't about his imminent death but about the loss of a judgement time I had been counting on. He would never face his crimes against us, he would never hear my detailed, unflinching account of life without him, or rather a life built around a Devon-shaped hole, he would never be sorry. I wanted him prostrate and repentant, he couldn't die now, where was the fucking justice?

I flew to London from San Francisco with my baby in tow so that, with any luck, she would meet her grandfather for the first and last time. But by the time I got there he was recovered and in a rehabilitation facility, having lost motor functions and speech. The doctors were shocked, it was rare for a patient in his situation to pull through but I knew that he was both stubborn and a Jamaican and wouldn't give up easily. He didn't. I met him at his house with his fiancée and new kid, and my new kid. He was doing days at the rehabilitation place and nights at home. He was slow, he was patchy on his memory, he accused me of not coming to see him in the hospital and I swallowed my fury as his fiancée reminded him where I lived and how far I had flown to see him.

In our hourlong conversation where he held my beautiful child, his first grandchild, I realised that although he hadn't died my chance at justice had indeed vanished. He couldn't remember a lot of things, and probably pretended he didn't remember more. I realised the work that I had hoped to do with him on our relationship I would have to do alone. Which was nothing new, but it still stung.

But you knew all of this. I didn't talk of my father too much but you knew about the heroin and the disappointment and the endless, endless pain. Is this why you never told me? Did you know that it would be too much for me?

In lieu of a frank and lengthy conversation with my father, I speak often with my mother. I am close with her in a nice and candid way, we can talk straight most of the time, I can ask questions of her that I know would make other parents bristle. She is fallible and mostly honest about her fallibility.

My father was using for the entire five years they were married.

The story I grew up knowing was that he was using, my mum couldn't have that around her kids and so they got divorced. Fin. The story I know now from long, chronicle-like conversations with her is different. He was using the entire time, yes, but she didn't know. She didn't know like I didn't know that Larissa was using—we both have the benefit of hindsight that allows us to now say, aha, yes, there it is. Hold the evidence, the late nights, the money requests, the sleepiness, the moodiness, the constant moving, up to the light like photo negatives to see it for what it is.

Sometimes we say to each other how stupid we feel for not seeing it. I still feel stupid.

My father lied endlessly to my mum. Barefaced lies. For years. Being lied to by the person you love and trust most in the world is exactly as destructive as you would imagine. My mum once said to me, "He lied so much that towards the end I would put my hand on the kitchen table and be unable to tell whether it was solid or not." She was crazed with uncertainty. She had no experience with heroin users, didn't know what to look for. She, like me, knows what to look for now. The damage my dad did to her mind was extensive, and it made her a distrusting and accusatory mother, which was suffocating to me (and my brother, I assume, although I have never asked him). It took her the length of my childhood and many, many therapy sessions to find a way through that suspicion, that inability to read what was in front of her. She is a different mother now.

I see so many parallels between my mother and father's relationship and mine and Larissa's. We loved each other deeply, one was afraid to tell the reality of their life and the other was too blind to the reality to help. My mother's experience with my father helped me see that it would have been impossible to save Larissa, despite my deep desire to have done so. We have made drug abuse so taboo, so disgusting, so reprehensible that the people who suffer from it often cannot safely do that one first step AA insists upon—admitting there is a problem. We have made it so that once you have put a needle into your arm you have been swept aside with the garbage, irredeemable and unforgivable. I didn't tell anyone until very recently that my dad was a heroin addict because I was so afraid of the stigma it would bring me. I almost didn't write of Larissa's struggle for the same reason, afraid of what her mother would think, but what good does it do to sweep it away? Where has that gotten us, and them?

Larissa was not an addict to me and so I will not represent her as one and in doing so I hope and believe that I am preserving her humanity, her complexity, her beauty and heart and love because she was so much more than the drugs she did. And I know that if that drug hadn't killed her, it wouldn't have fixed the problem. I still wouldn't have known what to do. I may have continued to be unable to see what was in front of my face, to say if the table was solid or not. It is wishful thinking (that I indulge in frequently) to believe something would have shifted. She didn't tell me, wouldn't have told me, for whatever reasons she didn't tell any of us. I would have continued to occasionally send her money and voice notes and we would have had our evergreen friendship but there would have been that dirty little secret tucked away in there somewhere and it wasn't for me to solve then and it isn't now.

I have lost both my dead best friend and my living father to heroin. For a long time, and sometimes still in the quiet of the night, I thought of myself as an idiot because what kind of person would have a heroin addict as a father and not see what was happening to their beloved friend? But now I know the insidiousness of the drug, the shame it carries, the desperation of the victim to still be the person we think of them as, hence the reluctance to just give in and tell us. If Larry had told me back then that she was using, how would I have reacted? With compassion? With patience? Or would I have unleashed all of the shit upon her that I could never subject my father to? Would she have become a proxy for him? Would I have driven her back into the shadows?

Now that the unthinkable has happened and my beautiful girl is dead, I have had the time to be angry and sad and shocked and devastated and finally, understanding of her in a way I am not sure I would have been able to if she had lived. Obviously not a trade-off I am thrilled with but it is a way to, at the end of a life, say to one I have loved most, I see you, I love you with it all, I understand, I forgive you, I'm sorry.

Eirinie <eirinieeee@xmail.com>   Aug 9, 2011
to Larissa

Larissa I really hope youre ok.
I love you so much please be safe
xxxxxxxxxx

Larissa <larry67@xmail.com>   Aug 9, 2011
to me

Omg seriously so much bullshit - OF course
I'm OK! Riots shmiots.
There's really nothing happening just
don't watch the news. All hype I
tell you! Miss you xxxxx

Eirinie <eirinieeee@xmail.com>   Aug 9, 2011
to Larissa

i miss you terribly.
What shall i do without my shmoomles?
Love of my life, light of my day!
xxxx

FORGIVENESS

There's a deeper understanding now, perhaps because I have discovered the secret door of a very private person. A very compartmentalised person. And now I have an overview, and with this knowledge I can comprehend her choices more.

Should I feel angrier? Should I feel sadder about how she died? Perhaps. But I don't. For me, finding out that she had died from heroin, finding out that she had kept this secret until it had killed her, it was like finding the final puzzle piece. I slotted it into the gaping space and said "ohhhhh" and I understood. Suddenly it made sense to me. Suddenly it contextualised a lot of the haze of the last few years of loving her. Jarring scenes of our friendship had meaning now, I knew now that her emails to me for money were because of the drugs, just as I knew that my reluctance to give it to her, my nagging sense that something was wrong, was because somewhere in my subconscious I knew what was happening. Yes, it is sad to think of all the ways I could have helped her if only I

had been allowed to see this before she died, yes, I think it incredibly frustrating that she never felt she could share this with me, this
considerable portion of her life . . . but I also understand, because
I knew her. I knew her like I know very few people, I knew her
intricacies and her thought patterns so well, without even asking.
And so, to have this piece of evidence introduced so late in the
trial, it feels like that one portion of Larissa that she would never
let me see, never let anyone see, was being revealed to me. A deeper
knowledge of her, a growth in our friendship albeit posthumously.
My god, that's who you are, Larissa. That's who you are and you're
still so beautiful, still so important, still so treasured to me.

Is this forgiveness?

Is it my right to forgive her, and if so, what am I forgiving her for?
For having a secret? For being a more complex person beyond my
knowledge of her? It feels something like forgiveness, but perhaps
that's what the acceptance stage of grief is. I forgive you. I forgive
you for dying. I understand it now and I am okay with it. I won't
rage against your absence anymore, I will endeavour to keep you
close, this new you, this revealed you. I will love you because of all
that you were and not in spite of it. I will remember you honestly,
I will look on unshrinkingly, I will not lie on your legacy. There is
no shame in who you were. My beautiful girl, my radiant friend, I
see through your darkness now and I will be there for you, even if
it seems too late. Because being your friend did not end when you
died. I am yours 'til the end of my days, and beyond, it may turn out.

This grief is lonely. I know what to do on your birthday now, it hit me like lightning, it's so obvious. A bottle of champagne, the good stuff, and a cigarette. A pack would be preferable but I could never handle them like you could. So just one, just a few drags, will be all I can give you.

I'll do it by myself, in the backyard when my kids are asleep. I'll do it alone because my mourning, here in America, is lonely. It is an island of grief. Surrounded by people who don't care or don't know what a loss your death is.

It is cathartic for me to share everything about Larissa. For me it is important to be as truthful as possible because now I fully understand that secrets can kill you. Of course, there are plenty of ways people die with an addiction out in the open, people die even when the people who love them are doing absolutely all they can to stop them from doing so. But surely in telling the truth loud, in showing the complexity of this special person, I can shed some of that taboo, some of that shame that keeps people like Larissa in the dark with their pain? I don't know. Is this a justification? Am I only saying this now because I am so truly worried about what her mother will think of it all?

Sometimes I get a tingle worrying what you'd think of all this, Larissa.

How would you feel if you could see what I was writing, what I was sharing? Am I being unreasonable, is this not okay? But it's my story too, this is my thing too. Unlike those shit sweaters and pieces of jewelry that I cannot recall ever seeing you wear, this is solely mine. This is not something to be divided amongst friends, no one can say "Hold on a minute, I want to say something" because these are my recollections, my thoughts, my emails, mine mine mine. I have finally staked out a little patch of earth for myself, and I may plant the seeds you left me. And this is what they have grown, this book, these words, these tears that still fall for you. My own little ecosystem, my own little microclimate, just you and I. You always were a hothouse flower for sure, not delicate exactly but particular. And I was so good at reading you, so good at being your constant gardener.

Maybe you'd understand. Maybe you'd get it, if you read it. You'd probably prefer our life story written in the form of a poem, but that was always more your realm than mine. I like to think, now that I've come this far, now that the majority of our friendship together has been mapped (because inevitably some has slipped through my fingers like water as I desperately tried to catch it all in my cupped hands), you'd see it. Like looking at a model of a city that you know so well, a city whose streets and roundabouts and parks and bus stops are so known to you that you barely even see them anymore, suddenly laid out before you in miniature, making so much sense and seeming so much more beautiful than you could have imagined. The buildings in which you were rejected or broken up with or laughed or cried in seem so small. It makes those moments seem just as small. It contextualises your blip of an existence in this vast place. And look! There's the river! Cutting through it all, a vein, an artery you crossed so many times on various bridges and now there it is, bluer than you remember it being, and beautiful now that you can't see all those filthy seagulls, all that garbage, all that baggage. I have zoomed out on our friendship and it spans further than we could have imagined, it is more nuanced and delicate and detailed and it is so worth all of the words, all of the tears, all of the pain and soul-searching it took to get this on a page.

Will your mother see it like this? Will she understand the relief in it? I truly hope so. I truly hope she'll understand that what we had, and what I've tried to lay out in this book, like a picnic blanket on a parched desert, is a portion of the country of you, the country of Larissa. Here you are in all your beauty and hideousness and meanness and selfishness and capacity for love and hilarity and intelligence. All the good and the bad, all of the skylines. I couldn't edit it out for her, it wouldn't have been true it wouldn't have been what I know.

You contained multitudes. I was but one portion of your life and so that is all I can speak on but here it is, my slice, my borough, my little bit of earth.

Is this all for your mother? I worry that she will be disgusted with my candid telling of secrets, that she won't understand or believe the sincerity of my intentions. It is not my aim to shame her family, it is not my aim to desecrate Larissa's memory, it is not my aim to make a spectacle. I just wanted to be honest. I just wanted to do what felt truthful to Larissa's story. I tried my best to tell it, ripe and lush and sweet like a peach, avoiding the hard pit in the centre, but it didn't feel true and it didn't feel good. Who am I helping if I hush up something that doesn't deserve to be hushed up? Who am I helping if I pile on a blanket of shame? Not the millions of people struggling with substance abuse or their family and friends. No. Not that this book is a crusade for them, it is a crusade for her. The unveiling of the truth should be righteous, a balancing of the scales, a rubbing of the eyes to see the full picture.

Larissa <larry67@xmail.com>   May 17, 2012
to me

i miss NY
when r we going there?

CHAPTER 38

AN ENDING, SORT OF

Almost three years since I lost you. Lately I've been thinking about that trip to the beach we took in New York. We went to Far Rockaway, we swam in the ocean together, kicking our legs and moving to keep afloat, laughing between mouthfuls of salt water. Sandy on the shore, tired and spent, dreading the long subway ride back. A rare day with you as you were not much of an active participant in anything. You usually preferred to sit on the shore and watch and wave, safe in your solitude.

Before you died, we talked a lot of New York and of going back. A halfway point for me in San Francisco and you in Paris, a quick time warp back into the depths of our history, back to hot nights of debauchery, back to our little conspiratorial bubble. We never got to go, but luckily for me so many of my memories of you are framed by that city and I know when I go back you will be there waiting for me, forcing me to visit your cheesy landmarks—Katz's Deli, Central Park, Carrie's Upper East Side apartment, a pilgrimage for you and for me.

My grief still comes in waves but now it is less tidal; I don't get pulled out to sea every time. Sometimes I am able to sit with my sorrow, to message Natalia or Maddy or Pierre, someone with whom I don't have to explain the nuances. Someone who will laugh knowingly when I talk of you leaving your *SATC* DVDs running in your room while you slept, so that everyone else in the flat had to listen to the DVD menu and its quotes on a loop: "Is your vagina in the New York City guidebook? Coz it should be! It's the hottest place in town, it's always open!"

Three years in I am starting to realise I will never be clean again, never be untainted by the loss of you, my sorrow has set in but not spread. I am the hull of a boat, rotten but seaworthy, holding steady despite my structural damage. I carry you with me, my passenger for always. And who can deny the sweetness of your company? The joy, the delight, the wisdom, the weirdness, the wholeness of you? Even in your absence I feel it.

Now, three years in, I can see the pattern of this thing, the wood for the trees. I know now that some days I shall be blithely unaware of my pain, the moss will have grown over the wound in my heart, I shall sing and dance and laugh and be happy or even be sad and angry and confused but I will not feel your loss. And when I finally come to from that burst of other feelings, I will also come back to the one true constant in my life now—I miss you, I love you, I wish what happened had never happened.

The regret of not having done more haunts me, even as I talk through its illogicalness with my therapist, admit that yes you were a person brilliant at segmenting your life and it was near impossible to get you to reveal anything you didn't want told. It was a delicate balance, extracting information from you or making you do something you weren't fully on board with, a tiptoeing as if around a deer drinking from a lake, one wrong move and you'd bolt noiselessly into the shrubbery and beyond. Once, when I was dating Adam and I still lived in London, I forced you to have dinner with me, Charlie and Adam. I so wanted you there that I had stopped caring if you actually wanted to go. You sulked throughout dinner, which was a fiasco as we hadn't bargained for long queues for a table, terrible service when we finally got into the restaurant, an unpleasant meal made more unpleasant by your surliness. I did my trick of paying for dinner before we were finished eating so that we could dash out into the night. I had thought if I made you come you would reluctantly have a good time but instead, we stonily stared at each other until you got in a cab, leaving the rest of us to discuss your behaviour over drinks at an Islington bar.

Thinking of this story, I know there is no way I could have made you tell me how sad you were, how scared, how broke, how ostracized. You would never have told me, even if I asked point-blank (which, looking back at our WhatsApp conversations, I see that I did several times) if everything was okay, if you needed anything. You died as you lived, clutching secrets unknown except to the privileged few who bore witness to that specific chapter. Initially

I blamed what happened to you and what led up to what happened to you on your ex, Pierre. But then, after that impromptu wake, when he walked me back to my flat, we talked of you for the whole two-mile journey. He told me things I never before knew, things I'd wanted to know, he patiently answered my questions, admitted when he didn't know anything. I realised, as we talked in those hushed voices reserved for midnight walks through sleeping neighbourhoods, that he did not damn you any more than I could have saved you.

Maybe it was your time to go. Maybe it was like that dinner and many other events you bailed on before, maybe I could never have made you stay, maybe you'd been pulling away the whole time but we had not been paying attention. Even if this is just like so much of what I say about you—an oversimplification of something deeper, something more complex because you can never ever really know all of anyone—it is comforting to remind myself that my power is in the letting go of you, the reimagining of you and not the ability to keep you here.

Because really who is to say that you are gone? Who can truly say that when I see those goddamn white butterflies everywhere, when I hear your songs in the most unlikely of places, when sometimes I catch myself laughing in that jarring, too-loud way you did, or when I find myself twirling the air with my fingertips whilst I search for a word as you did, or the feeling of you close when I am alone in the night drinking a particularly good glass of red? Is that not you? Is my thinking of you, my conjuring, not just you but in a different form? Maybe you're right here with me as I type, kind laughter as you watch me realise that the universe is not limited to my knowledge of it.

I know that I could not have saved you. I know that because I never saved you before, it was always you saving me. And you're saving me all over again as you help me figure this shit out, saving me from drowning in my own tears, saving me by letting me know we never truly die.

You feel close, Larry. You feel so close it has to be real.

Would I have felt this epiphany, this reimagining, without allowing myself to feel the pain of your absence? If I had buried it deep only to have it one day burst forth like an unsanctioned geyser, coming too thick and fast to control? Probably not. It is only after nearly three years of grappling with my grief and turning it over and over like an unusual stone found by the shore that I can see its facets and fractures.

And if time is just a flat circle, if we relive these moments over and over and over again, palimpsests of the past beneath the outline of the future, perhaps it is fair to say that we are still in Far Rockaway, on that beach, toes nestled between sand and pebbles, the tide pulling our legs out with it, laughing and thinking of nothing except the right-now-ness of it all.

ACKNOWLEDGEMENTS

Every book I ever write will end with a thank-you to one of my best friends and trusted writing partner, Steph Tataryn. *The Dead Are Gods* wouldn't have existed without you, you have been an inspiration and a catalyst and a voice of reason more times than I can count. You read the first iteration of this book, a small essay written in the depths of a sadness I couldn't get out of, and you said, simply, "More. Give me more." You said that over and over and over again until I had an agent, a complete book, and a publisher. You have a distinct stylistic eye and a talent for pulling the best out of the people you love; you know what you like and whom you love and lucky for me I am one of them. Thank you, Steph, my champion.

To my husband, Adam. Whenever people ask how on earth I wrote a whole book during a pandemic with one (and later, two) children, I point to you. You are a man who is generous with his time, who respects the work I do even when it looks like lying on the floor trying to think of synonyms for "dead." An artist, a shit-hot drummer, a dedicated father; life without you would lack any centre, purpose, or grounding.

To Larissa's lifelong friends Madeleine Dunbar and Natalia Rodriguez, who graciously agreed to be my early readers, who gave me honest and kind feedback and made me feel safe in the knowledge that I had done right by our girl. Thank you.

To my mum, a powerhouse grafter of a woman, who has been telling me to keep writing since I finished "Relative Blunders," who is frustratingly right about most things, oh look, you were right! Right about writing! Thank you for the push. Thank you for being proud of me and letting me know and feel it often.

To my late grandfather, the inimitable Patrick Reyntiens, who read me *Beowulf* when I was nine years old, who had a personal library of cherry-picked books that became my happy place, thank you for supporting my love of reading. Thank you for thinking I was something special.

To Danielle Svetcov for putting me onto my phenomenal agent Tim Wojcik, who took a chance on a green-as-fuck writer who sends too many emails, thank you. To Tim, a chill and funny and tenacious person to have on my team, thank you for support-ing me, always answering my texts, and laughing at my jokes. To Athena Bryan for taking a chance on a green-as-fuck writer and showing the team at Melville House my book so they could love it, thank you.

To Carl Bromley, a man whom I only ever full-name because it is so distinctly London, thank you for your considerate edit, your humour, and your prompt replies to vague and existential questions such as "What do I do now?"

To Callie Jacks, who helped me write the summary of this very book one late night in the Adirondacks, thank you for your cool, smart, young person's eye.

To Charlie Vaughan, Marissa Puget, Samantha Beagley, Kirby Stenger, Kate Faust, Markel Archie, Robyn Greene-Archie, Daesha Devón Harris, Jonny Santos, Shelly Romero, Ashley Batz, William Cozby, Jennifer Wakefield, Emma Dabiri, Davey Havok, Rosie Lowe, Sarah Rainey, Charlotte Grant, Phil Green, my Carson family (Amy, Will, Jeanie), Kailea Frederick, The SF Writers Grotto, Roberto Lovato—your encouragement and cheerleading and various contributions kept me going.

And to my babies. I treasure who you are so dearly, and I just know that Auntie Larissa would have loved you both. You have brought me more joy than I ever thought I deserved. Without you this book would have been finished a year ago.